Little Wheels

Across Australia in a Baby Austin

HECTOR MacQUARRIE

ETT IMPRINT
Exile Bay

First paperback edition published by ETT Imprint, Exile Bay 2025

First published as *We and the Baby* by Angus & Robertson, 1929

THE substance of this book first appeared in a series of articles in the *Sydney Mail*; and for permission to reproduce them here I am indebted to the proprietors of that journal. In particular, I find myself under a debt of gratitude to Mr. W. R. Charlton, the *Mail*'s editor, for his unfailing sympathy and good humour during the sixteen weeks in which *We and the Baby* wandered through his pages. H. M.

Copyright © ETT Imprint 2025

This book is copyright. Apart from any fair dealing for the purposes of private study, research, criticism or review, as permitted under the Copyright Act, no part may be reproduced by any process without written permission. Enquiries should be addressed to the publisher, or via this email ettimprint@hotmail.com

ETT IMPRINT
PO Box R1906
Royal Exchange NSW 1225 Australia

ISBN 978-1-923205-58-1 (paper)
ISBN 978-1-923205-60-4 (ebook)

Design by Tom Thompson

CONTENTS

HOW IT ALL BEGAN 6
OUR ADVENTURES BEGIN 15
IN AND AROUND CAIRNS 33
DARK FOREBODINGS 48
THE ATHERTON TABLELAND 57
GETTING WARMER 67
WE ATTACK THE BYERSTOWN RANGE 80
TARRED ROADS 95
HENRY'S TOOTH 116
COEN TO MEIN 131
MEIN AND ONWARDS 140
TO MORETON TELEGRAPH STATION AND ONWARDS 151
THE JARDINE! 163

TO MY SISTER MARGARET FINLAYSON
I dedicate this book in a poor attempt to show her how much I love her.

Betty Gunn, one of the five inhabitants of the Cape York Telegraph Station, atop our Baby Austin.

1

How It All Began

IT began like this:

Dick came in from his little home town of Kaitaia in the north of New Zealand to my big town of Auckland. "Well," said he, "when are we going?"

"Going where?" I asked.

"Oh," he returned with a careless gesture taking in the possible world - "to Peru or Chile or somewhere! Wherever we're going to!"

"We'll go to-night, if you like," I laughed, leading him in to tea -" let's fly there!"

At that moment it seemed as easy to fly to South America as it would be to pay our fares there.

"Don't you realize, old man," I continued, when I had got him inside, "don't you realize that it takes money to travel? We're both about broke. I'm looking for a job!"

He was silent. But not for a second was I deceived into a condition of false security. Dick is slightly more articulate than a landslide when he wants anything; and as effective, too, when he wants to carry me with him. Obviously he had decided to go gadding about the world; it was equally obvious that he had decided to seduce me into joining him. I had already given in; but I was interested in watching his tactics. It seemed necessary, too, for the elder friend to give good advice; so I dished him up a little compote of what I so often receive.

"You see, my dear old chap," I said brightly; "a rolling stone gathers no moss. I'll admit *that's* been said before; but moss is necessary, if it's only to line your grave with. If you go wandering about the world now, you'll be unsettled for the rest of your life. You may have some fun, but when all your contemporaries are rich and prosperous you'll be poor. No, no! you go back to your father's sheep; work hard, and I'll bet you he'll give you the place within five years. Then, with plenty of money in your pockets and a good wife on your arm, you can travel on a Cook's ticket!"

"Eggs-zactly!" said Dick, quoting a mutual friend.

"You may," I pursued, "have the middle-age spread and fat jowls; but better an overdraft in your abdomen than one your banker won't give you. A good figure's important at forty-as long as it's in your pass-book!"

(I've had all the above - even the jokes!)

"They gave me a great farewell in Kaitaia," said Dick slowly.

"A farewell!" I echoed.

"And presented me with a leather suit-case at the dance. People made speeches, and I promised to write to half-a-dozen. I wrote out a speech before the dance and lost it. But I remembered a good deal, and said it off from memory - not bad, really! It was a great night."

Dick said little more. He has not said a great deal since. Having effectively wound me up with the awful threat of an anti-climax, he was content, and has remained content, to let me do all the talking. We had certainly discussed trips to different places, but they were, I thought, hardly more than dreams. They were probably the kind of dreams which are being dreamt all over the world at this minute by ardent souls tied to office desks or chained by responsibility - dreams of travel and adventure in the wide, wide world. If by any chance a fellow-dreamer should read these lines of mine, let him watch us closely! I am writing for him. Because I know he would not like us to lie or bound, I am going to be very candid.

I recalled, that night, while Dick was waiting for me to give in, how hopelessly undecided we had been upon one occasion. A trip to Peru and a trek down through South America collecting golden relics left in caves and grottos by the ancient Incas had seemed to have great possibilities; but a motor-cycle journey from southern Italy to England, selling something or other to pay expenses, and taking in an audience with the Pope had been equally attractive. We had turned in without reaching a decision, and I, at least, had forgotten the matter the next day. They were safe dreams to dream, I knew, because we were both enduring a financial slump.

But here was Dick getting farewelled at Kaitaia and already started on his journey. He was certain I would not fail him. With complete faith he had burnt his bridges, knowing full well that I would never see him return to his small town with that suit-case in his hand while the tears of his friends were undried. I will always shy at an anti-climax.

Although I had given in, I was not eager to leave Auckland at that time. Loved ones seemed to be getting a bit old; one, my mother, had not been resting for very long in the churchyard across the bay from where I lived, and it was nice to be near her on Sunday afternoons, nicer, perhaps, in some ways because I had not been with her a great deal latterly - the war years, followed by others having been spent in wandering about the world! I had, too, a small Australian terrier called Typee, whom I liked being with; my immense Persian cat, who held a daily reception (of passers-by) on the rockery near the gates, had definitely decided to endure me as his second master (the cook being his first) and rather liked me. I was in the throes of designing and building a most attractive fernery with a goldfish pond in its centre. Moreover, a new car had replaced the old phaeton in what was immediately called the garage, and its owner had suggested that if I were a very good boy I might, a little later on, be taught to drive it, and even be permitted to take it out on the chauffeur-gardener's days off. She, this loved one who owns the car, thinks I am still eighteen and feckless. Much water has passed under the bridge since I was eighteen, thank God! Indeed, a lady in New Guinea said a few months ago, when I had frivolously and lyingly confessed to twenty-five. Huh! I'd hate like hell to have been hanging by the neck since you were twenty-five! I fear she would be excessively dead!

To return to that July evening in Auckland.

Dick wanted to go adventuring; I decided to go with him.

"The only thing to do now," I said finally, "is to go out and see Jack and Doreen."

Jack and Doreen are a pair of birds who live in a handsome nest some two or three miles out of Auckland. They twitter on various keys and have young. Jack is the chief partner in a very prosperous motor company; but great business success has not in any way affected his boundless enthusiasm in other directions. A few days earlier, having met an old friend home on leave from Malay, he had picked up the Straits Settlements, immediately reading up everything he could find on the place. Well and truly stoked, I knew he was ready to puff out powerful steam on the Straits. He had never succeeded in convincing anyone of the advisability of instantly packing up and making for Malaya; I doubt if he wanted to. The jolly living-room at Orakei which he shares with Doreen and his baby is merely a debating-hall to Jack, in which he gains points.

He was rather astonished, and I think secretly distressed, when Dick and I admitted the soundness of all his arguments and said we would sail for Malaya by the first steamer.

The Malay idea was not a bad one. We both had plenty of friends with friends in the Straits. We managed, with some difficulty, to rake together enough money to pay our fares, and there would be a little over for emergencies. There seemed no doubt but that we should find employment within a reasonable time; and then, should we dislike the place, we could always return.

But the demon of mischief or adventure - or was it a more benignant spirit? - entered my allegedly cautious head as we were walking up Symond's Street to see our friend Jack in his office a few days before we left Auckland. "Dick," I said; "in looking at a big map of Australia this morning it seemed to me rather futile to make all that journey up the coast of Australia in a mere steamer."

"What other way is there? " he asked.

"I don't know," I replied; "but there's all that wonderful country of New South Wales, and the whole of Queensland rising right up to near New Guinea and ending at Cape York. The Australia of Sydney, Melbourne, and Brisbane I know; I should like to know something of that hot tropical part where there are crocodiles and wild natives - where the new Australia we know something of meets the old world of the Orient! "

"It sounds very interesting," said Dick; "let's have it! What's the big idea?"

"What about buying a secondhand motor-truck in Sydney and caravanning our way right up to Cape York, then selling the truck at a big profit - they'd be sure to buy it and be glad of it - and then getting across to Thursday Island and picking up the liner there?"

"A damn good idea," said Dick; "let's!"

It will be observed that Dick and I invariably foresaw great profits in all our schemes. It never occurred to us that the Cape York Peninsula might be largely uninhabited and therefore roadless. We became wildly enthusiastic, and hurried to Jack's office to unfold our scheme.

"Magnificent!" Jack exclaimed; "I'll write you a letter at once to our agents in Sydney; they might give you one of their small cars to do it in."

Within a few minutes a typist had appeared, and Jack was lying most eloquently. Dick and I were intrepid motorists; and, if anything, I was more intrepid than Dick. My old military title was shamelessly revived, and it was pointed out to the Sydney agents that, if they succeeded in persuading us to accept one of their trucks or cars, they would be very lucky agents indeed.

"D'you realize, Jack," I said, "that I have never driven a car in my life and don't particularly want to?"

"Dick'll teach you," returned Jack," let's have a drink while the girl does the letter."

All our friends came to the wharf to bid us good-bye. Dick had a small circle of kissing ladies and hand-shaking men; I had the same. My big white Persian had scratched so many people and things when encouraged to travel in the car to see me off that they abandoned him with curses at the gates; but Typee, who loved cars, was on the seat with the chauffeur. When I endeavoured to lift him up, he growled - Typee was never a serf - and so I nestled my head in his silky coat and bade him be a good little man until I returned. Alas, Typee refused to wait more than a month for me; he gave up his doggy ghost then, and I still mourn for him. If I ever reach Heaven I shall expect to find Typee there, attempting to rule it over the other angel dogs, notably those much bigger than himself, who are too chivalrous (or puzzled) to suppress him.

We reached Sydney and settled on my beautiful sister, who lives there. She had no objections, and not much room; and so we were all happy together.

Eventually we presented our letter to the car agents. Jack has a fine reputation in the motor world, and we were therefore taken much more seriously than we deserved. We were placed in the hands of the firm's publicity officer, who was ordered to do his best for us. He did. He rushed us around Sydney, introducing us to all kinds of agents interested in British cars and trucks; but although he presented me again and again as "an intrepid motorist," we made little headway. I wanted to use a Baby Austin; but those who knew, or who thought they knew, decided that this car would be much too light for the job. I could not agree. When Dick and I were founding the village called Pandora in Spirit's Bay, near the northerly end of New Zealand (we are the proud fathers of Pandora, which we named; it can now be seen on modern maps) Jack drove a Baby Austin down into the village, months before the road was completed. The little car came down the precipitous slopes of the valley on a sheep-pad. Our fat old horse "Counter," and our Maori man Bob, and we ourselves hung on to the little car and prayed; but I believe she would have managed the job herself.

Finally, we were offered a half-ton Ford truck for £37 10s. The greengrocer who owned it was retiring, and his reputation was of the best. We decided to buy this caravan if the Austin agents refused to meet us with one of their sevens. They had no desire in the world to refuse us anything within reason; but after careful inquiry they had discovered that the main highway of eastern Australia ended not far north of Cairns; they could not see how any car could negotiate the remaining five or six hundred miles to Cape York over dangerous roadless country. However, before deciding, they introduced me to a very great person, himself a British motor agent, who knew something of the country.

"I hear you propose to motor from Sydney to Cape York," said this gentleman.

"Yes," I replied carelessly. I fear my tone was a trifle petulant; I was getting extremely bored with the amused opposition we were enduring.

"Then," said he very seriously, "I am bound to tell you that I was interested in an expedition to an old tin-mine near Shelbourne Bay, about a hundred miles south of Cape York. We landed a car - a much better car for the job than you propose to take, with a chain drive-and they pushed inland about fourteen miles. That journey, over what had once been a road, occupied more than three weeks. The car had three white men, a Japanese, and several aborigines with it. The expedition found a white man, starving. They were too late to save him. He died!"

Secretly, I shuddered. I said, "Dear me - poor fellow! What did he die of?"

"Starvation," said the gentleman; "beyond a few wild yams and cockatoos there is no natural food in the peninsula."

My question may seem a little absurd in view of the fact that I had been told of the man's starving condition; but actually, and of course by by chance, it was a good enough question which I can answer now. "The man died of gall-stones, which neither Dick nor I have - so far"; and he had been dying within the memory of the oldest inhabitant of the North. He had, poor fellow missed supplies of suitable food through the seasonal rains which came too early or remained too long. We better passed not very far inland from his grave; we also passed not very far from the grave of that "much car for the job!" The gentleman was obviously doing his best for us; he was depending upon reports, and he actually knew very little.

"Now you," pursued my friend, "propose to motor, not fourteen miles, but half a thousand. Of course, I know you're an efficient driver - !"

"Do you?" I thought, but I simply made a modest kind of gesture, and the gentleman continued:

"You can't," he said, "drive across eighty rivers and countless creeks, to say nothing of hills and mountains -"

I might have explained that I couldn't drive across a tennis-court, but we wanted to get an Austin seven, and so I merely eventually smiled.

"The rivers are dry, true," he went on; "but that makes them worse - simply mighty gulches with steep sides! There is little water; snakes are plentiful; crocodiles are not scarce; the aborigines are said to be dangerous, and the country over hundreds of miles is uninhabited. There are, of course, no roads! "

"And yet," I said, "we will go!"

Which sounds very brave of me. It was, actually, the courage of desperation. Sydney had proved most alluring to our pocket-book. I doubt if we then had enough money to pay our fares to Singapore. We simply had to get an Austin seven cheaply from the agents, or the second-hand Ford truck from the greengrocer; we had to reach Cape York; and we had to sell either the car or the truck at a profit. I am amazed to realize at this moment that we carried out every intention to the letter. We now know, as we suspected then, that no one in Sydney knew anything about the extreme north of the continent. We were certain that a way would be found.

We finally reached an arrangement with the car agents. We agreed to make a substantial deposit on the purchase of a Baby Austin and to insure it in the name of the agent. That came to something over £60. We agreed to supply the agents with information and photographs as we progressed. If we reached Cape York, the car became our property. It was not decided what would happen if we failed. A car which had been used by a salesman, but a very good one, was given to us, and we began making preparations for the long journey.

I want, if possible, again to stress the points that (a) we had to reach Cape York and (b) the car had to remain in first-class condition - all paintwork fresh-looking and the engine running sweetly. No one will buy a car with rusty scratched sides; no one wants a car with an ill-treated engine. We had to sell that car on Thursday Island at a price not far short of its full selling price in Sydney.

It was now necessary to see what could be done with newspapers. In the working out of expenses we had calculated upon selling at least a dozen articles. We had no great success. We found no one in Sydney willing to take us seriously. Certainly the editor of the *Sydney Morning Herald* agreed to consider any articles I sent - journalists will appreciate the importance of that - but it was impossible to make serious contracts. There was no news value in the first traverse of the Cape York Peninsula by car. And, like the great peninsula, Dick and I were unknown, and not important. The few newspaper people who gave the matter the slightest consideration thought us silly, rather than mad or foolhardy, to make the attempt. And yet, historically, the Cape York Peninsula is the oldest part of Australia. Imagine its significance in the event of war in the Orient! And I haven't the slightest doubt but that the passing of a few years will see the projection of a fine road from the heavily-populated south to the north. Days of weary sea-travel and much time will be saved for people travelling to the East, and even to Europe.

I must continue to bore a little longer by explaining our preparations. We could afford no spares; and we took a serious chance here. Beyond the usual spare wheel and a few secondhand wheel-spokes, we carried no spares. Later we were lent an extra magneto. A friend gave us a square of tarpaulin. Mr. Moss, who makes car-hoods and spare-wheel covers and all that kind of thing for motors, in Sydney, turned our tarpaulin into a fine little tent which would run from the side of the car. He fitted stout linen pockets to the doors. He made a magnificent spare-wheel cover for us and painted "Sydney to Cape York" on it. He turned an old car-hood into a fine waterproof sheet for us. He covered our three-ply tucker-box, fitted to the running-board, with waterproof material, and he completed our equipment with a camp griller. When moved, Mr. Moss stutters very attractively; hence when I had asked him for his bill and he had refused to give us one, and we had expressed our gratitude, he said, closing his lips tightly, "I'm g-g-g-g-lad!" And we knew he was.

Dick was all for dashing up to Cape York in little more than a bathing-suit; but I insisted on a suitcase of respectable clothing to wear in the towns of the inhabited country. The suitcase could be left at Cairns and later shipped to Thursday Island. We carried a small typewriter with which to write the articles (none of them sold), a stoutish volume of Shakespeare, and *Alice in Wonderland*.

My sister made herself responsible for the fitting out of the tucker-box, which soon held decent china cups and saucers, good cutlery and plate, and even a Royal Doulton teapot with cherries and grapes painted on it." Tut, tut !" I said, when I saw this lovely vessel getting stowed in the tucker-box; " didn't your church present that to you for good works? Why part with it?" "It's got," she said, "a worse delivery than a tongue-tied parson!" It had. The niece gave us a linen tablecloth with a border of red, yellow, and blue. I don't know what was the matter with it; we still use it. She also packed our car exquisitely, so exquisitely that, whenever we found anything, it was in the nature of a triumph. On the whole we were beautifully fitted out when we started; and we kept beautiful for quite a long while.

Having packed our box with a shoulder of lamb, with a salad and dressing, with pots of soup, jam, and honey - generally with enough provisions to keep us happy for a day or two - my beautiful sister ran away and hid. She could not bear the parting. And yet she has never forgiven us for sending her a wire from Brisbane when we reached that town. She had invested five shillings in the Queensland Golden Casket, and it was drawn the day before we reached Brisbane. My sister's joy in knowing we had reached Brisbane was therefore swamped in an awful anti-climax. A telegram from Brisbane that day could only tell her she'd won the £5,000.

I do not propose to deal with the story of our adventures very much south of Cairns. We enjoyed that journey thoroughly; but it is a way often followed by motorists, and I have nothing new to say. I may add that we dawdled our way up the coast. We were guarding the car tenderly, preparing her for surely the greatest test any car has ever been asked to face.

2
Our Adventures Begin

"If it's natural for the kangaroo to have its young born in its pouch, it will have its young born in its pouch, because it's Nature. And you can't go against Nature." -
Roy's Mate.

FIFTEEN hundred miles of our journey covered, and now a few miles south of the northern Queensland port of Townsville, we were motoring slowly along the coast road in a cloud of dust stirred up by Townsvillians making for home from the Ayr races. It was Saturday evening, and getting unpleasantly late. At five o'clock we had found a good enough camping-ground near a passable lagoon-like creek, but, hoping for something better, and less attractive to crocodiles, we had pushed on. We always rested on Sundays whenever possible, and the choice of a good spot was therefore of great importance. We required something special in the way of a running creek of clear water for bathing and washing clothes in. We were in the tropics now, and Dick needed the coolness of shady trees for his weekly dive under the car to examine her more intimate workings. I had found it very difficult to raise a good shine on enamel paint when the sun dried the polish a few seconds after it had been applied. I must add that, despite an awful gruelling on execrable roads farther south, the little car still remained perfectly fresh and new-looking. Holland loose covers protected the cushions and seats; our prospective buyer on Thursday Island (a rich creature of our dreams) had still every chance of driving a handsome little car.

    On we drove. It became dark. We were hungry and obviously very peevish. Townsville was drawing nearer every minute, and we had no desire to enter a town at night, when it would be necessary to spend money on hotel entertainment. Moreover, we had maintained a practice of never reaching a place looking intrepid. A few miles outside we invariably paused at a creek to clean and polish the car and ourselves, so as to enter a town looking smart enough for a garden party. No one ever asked us to a garden party, but we could have kept our ends up at one if anybody had.

    At last we saw a fire burning near the road.

    Two dark figures were apparently loading a small sugar-cane truck.

We turned our headlights on to the truck. "Now that's very nice of you," a deep musical voice shouted; "who the hell are you? "

"We're looking for a good camping-ground," I replied; "do you know of one? "

"Why yes, plenty," returned the voice; "wait until we've loaded this damn truck and we'll show you."

With the great help of our lights, the two men soon finished their task, and they came over to the car. It was too dark to distinguish faces; but we could easily see that both men were very big, averaging, I should think, about fourteen stone.

"Now don't move," said one; "we'll ride on the running-boards; it's not far; we'll take you over to our place."

I shuddered, and waited for Dick to object or to explain. The running-boards of our car were hardly more than tin. Dick weighs nearly twelve stone and I weigh ten. The back seat was piled high with baggage weighing about four hundred weight, and the total weight of the car was no more than eight hundredweight! She had stood up magnificently to this awful burden; and I had suffered considerably from Dick's reproaches. "Oh, it's cruel!" he used to say grimly when the grand little engine was struggling up steep pinches; but I would never consent to shipping our suitcase or jettisoning Shakespeare. I've got past the age of looking romantic in a dirty shirt, and although we never read Shakespeare there was always the chance that we might want to. Obviously, when these two giants attached themselves to the running-boards, the springs of the little car went flat. Nevertheless, Dick's fine driving over a bumpy side-road saved her from dissolution, and we reached our destination without an accident. I must add quickly that both men were seriously distressed the next morning when they appreciated the size of the car. "We thought," one said, "It was a motor-car!"

We were near a small cottage, but this was completely filled, the men explained, by the wife and family of one and the mother of the other. They led us to their own sleeping-quarters, a large rambling hut with bark sides and an iron roof. They called this a "humpy." Very soon a fire was blazing in an excellent stove; beds were arranged; and after a good meal of boiled eggs and brown bread we settled down to yarn.

It was still too dark to see our hosts clearly, for the hurricane-lantern hanging from the roof gave the poorest light, but I soon guessed that the two men were great friends and, as so often happens in friendship, not a bit alike. They were both about thirty-five, I guessed, and powerful, muscular men; but while the personality of one was compelling and warm, the other seemed minus and dull. One talked a great deal and seemed overflowing with hospitality; he was slightly bigger. The other said very little, although I must admit that when he did speak he spoke with awful effect.

The bigger man - presumably I must invent him a name - Roy Jackson, is well known throughout northern Queensland. I have heard him discussed. I have yet to meet anyone who dislikes him. The mention of his name invariably inspires a smile which has more liking and admiration in it than condemnation. I know he could be very dangerous if desperate, for he has little reserve and the strength of a tiger; but I could never imagine him being cruel or failing to help a lame dog over a stile. Given home life and a better education, Roy would have gone far. He has not done so badly as it is. He makes fortunes and loses them with equal facility. Apparently he is always dragging his mate out of trouble. He tried to show me how much he despised his plodding pal, but I saw only warm friendship and affection. He criticized him quite openly and a little comically.

"You can be quite certain," he said, "that Bill will do the wrong thing. He works like a nigger, but although I've started him on many good ideas, he always crashes - "

Bill came into the humpy at that moment, and, while he filled his pipe before retiring to a box in a dim alcove of the rambling old hut, Roy continued quite unconcernedly.

"He got married-five years ago," said Roy irritably. "Oh, that's all right; but when a fellow struggling on a sugar farm during bad seasons of drought has four children in rapid concussion there must be something wrong with him! His wife's face went out of shape when she had the last. One of her eyes is up on her forehead, now!"

Bill said nothing. I could see the calm intermittent glow of his pipe during the recital of this little history. Possibly he knew his Roy, although as I saw the next day, the history was not inaccurate.

I think we were something of a find to Roy Jackson; he enjoys talking, and we had many questions to ask. He had a very rich musical voice with a weary, blase cadence which was wholly restful. During his adventurous life he

Crossing the Mitchell River.

Recrossing the Mitchell River after being bushed.

had evidently kept his eyes open; he had the pleasing humility of the artist; he seldom attempted words he could not manage, and he was never pig-headed in a discussion. That night he was dressed in rough working-clothes, and he was seriously due for a shave, but I could imagine him making a handsome figure of a man when properly turned out. We began with marsupials.

The marsupial is described in the dictionary as "of the class of mammals that produce their young partly developed and carry them for a time in a pouch." But few bushmen in Queensland accept that. Many, if not all, hold that the marsupial young make their first bow to the world actually in the pouch. They are unable to explain precisely what happens. One old man near Rockhampton left me with the vague impression that an infant kangaroo grows from its own tongue and starts life like a fox's head on a tie-pin! He was quite fierce on the subject. Evidently the marsupial baby is very small when he is helped to the pouch by his parent's hand-like fore-paws. We had heard so much, and had previously known so little, that both Dick and I were in grave doubt. Nevertheless I felt that Science would not agree with Roy's contention that a young marsupial actually begins existence in the pouch, and I said so. Dick remained neutral. I think I made one or two good points; but the rich, weary voice continued to quote, and there seemed no way out.

And then, for the first time that evening, Roy's mate spoke - and we were annihilated! He had risen from his seat in the alcove and had come within the faint glow of the hanging lantern. Raising his eyebrows and pointing his pipe at us, he said:

"If it's natural for the kangaroo to have its young born in its pouch, it will have its young born in its pouch, because it's Nature. And -" very sternly - "you can't go against Nature!"

"Of course you can't go against Nature," I snapped impatiently, "who wants to? - but that's no argument. It's a -"

"Fact!" said Roy's mate impressively; "if it's natural for the kangaroo to have its young born in its pouch, it will have its young born in its pouch; because it's Nature. And, as I said - *You can't go against nature!*"

Bill returned slowly to his dim alcove. I glanced at Roy, observing that all the life had been crushed out of him, and so I decided to die with him on the marsupial subject.

We were strangely quiet for some minutes while I poured out tea from my sister's Doulton teapot. Finally I ventured to ask a few questions about crocodiles, and Roy was soon alive again. It has been explained to me so often which species is found in Australia that the process of running up and down the whole gamut of knowledge on the point has reduced me to utter ignorance when far from a book of reference. I met a man in Mackay who had a large crocodile and a fairly big alligator (brought from America) in his back yard ; he explained the difference. I do not know it now. However, I do know at this moment that only the crocodile is found in Australia. However, the people of the country where he lives persist in calling him an alligator when he is found not too far from the sea. Inland, in the deep pools of partially dry rivers, he is called a crocodile. A bushman will bogey (bathe) in the same pool with a crocodile without any fear; he won't swim within a mile of what he calls an alligator. There seems no doubt but that well inland, the reptile is harmless; and there is equally no doubt but that he is excessively dangerous near the coast. Only one species exists in Australia, I am assured - the crocodile! I repeat that; but I should crumple up instantly if anyone said I was wrong ! It would not be safe to say that to Roy. I did not say it because at that time I did not know. He told us one or two very lurid stories. This one I refuse to believe, but I might as well tell it.

Two bushmen encamped near the mouth of a stream removed their clothing and ran swiftly to a swimming-hole. The first dived in, but in mid-air, before reaching the water, shrieked, "Gator!" The second was naturally deterred, and waited in vain for the return to the surface of his mate. He rushed for help. Others came. They dynamited the hole, and very soon the mangled body of the first swimmer rose slowly to the surface. They drew it carefully out of the water and had succeeded in getting it on to the bank when a great "old man" crocodile emerged, roaring like a bull. Most of the men made off for their lives; but one automatically clung to the corpse, and by zigzagging he eventually outdistanced the reptile and got up a tree with the dead man. After a time the disappointed crocodile returned to the water-hole; and the dead man had a decent funeral.

That story, of course, is based on a false premise.

The crocodile is very shy, and very cunning in a heavy kind of way; no beast of prey goes hunting with a greater care for personal safety. He will often grab the head of a drinking beast, the leg of a careless bather, or the feet of a native woman searching for oysters and crabs in the mangroves; I have even heard of him upsetting canoes full of natives! at night-time in New Guinea; but generally he will not attack unless the odds in his favour are very heavy indeed.

Roy and I began discussing crocodile eggs. I knew that the female crocodile laid upwards of thirty eggs, and I had heard that she arranged her nest as far away as possible from the haunts of her husband, so that he might not be tempted to gobble up his children a few minutes after hatching. A man farther south had said that the female herself was not above enjoying a few of her young; but that I doubted. A fellow in Proserpine told us that he actually saw a large female crocodile shepherding some young down a river, making a bow with her immense tail along the river-bank. Roy said that the first little crocodiles to hatch out were the strongest, and fought and often killed and ate their dilatory sisters and brothers. I was. carefully avoiding anything approaching an argument; it seemed best to keep Roy's mate quiet; but very soon I was laying down the law about maternal instincts. I could not believe, I said, that the female crocodile ate her own young. Alas, we had worked up Bill again, and it was terrible.

"If," said he, again emerging from the gloom, "it's natural for the female crocodile to eat her young, she will eat them - because it's Nature! If it's natural for the male crocodile to fight his missus for the privilege, he will do so - because it's Nature. You can't go against Nature!" Bill borrowed more of our tobacco and withdrew to his alcove.

Roy and I were not quite so completely annihilated about crocodiles as we had been about marsupials, and we discussed the strange habits of other local beasts and birds without much of a pause. We even returned to crocodiles.

Dick and I had, of course, been carefully warned about these reptiles, but farther south, where they do not exist. In the country from Rockhampton northwards, where they abound, no one seemed greatly concerned, although precautions are always taken. I fear we became very careless, and hardly gave them a thought. The crocodile is, however, very interesting. It seems most amazing to realize that from an egg no bigger than a chicken's a monster sometimes thirty feet in length can grow. I understand that a crocodile lives for hundreds of years. Imagine it! The crocodiles in the streams we crossed may have cocked bleary eyes on Captain Cook ! I was told that every river area has an "old man" crocodile who is the " boss of the river"; younger bulls occasionally challenge him! The females, it is said, await the result with great interest.

Snakes do not seem to hibernate in tropic Australia, and the different species have apparently different months for coupling. A snake will usually glide off when disturbed if he can; but when coupling, the male at least is courageous, and will go out of his way to strike. I know of a brown snake attacking a horse carrying a stock-man. When the horse collapsed, the snake chased the man, and very nearly caught him.

However, although we slept on the ground over thousands of miles, and passed through country when certain species were coupling, we saw few snakes. We used mosquito nets, an excellent protection against snakes. Which sounds silly, but actually a well-tucked in net prevents snakes from nestling in one's blankets.

Roy warned us about the rough country to the north of us.

He had left his couch and was standing filling his pipe near the table under the dim hurricane-lantern. "You," he said to me a little accusingly, "are fresh from the Old Country!"

"I'm not!" I said stoutly; "I'm a New Zealander."

"Nevertheless," he went on, " you're going to be surprised. Take the case of Angus MacPhee who came down from Brickville!"

Roy pulled at his pipe. It was out, for, like most vocal people, he smokes matches. He dug out his matches and carefully lighted his pipe. I glanced at Bill a little fearfully, but he was not yet intellectually stimulated and apparently not ready to stress the natural conduct of the man from Brickville.

"Angus MacPhee came down from Brickville," continued Roy, "and pulled up at a small country pub. Angus was a great hairy man with a beard sticking out from his face and chest. His arms were like the hind-legs of bullocks, and his hands were the hands of a giant gorilla. He hadn't changed his shirt for a year, and you could smell him a mile off!"

Roy paused to see how we enjoyed this savoury description of Angus, and went on: "Hey, you -- little bitch! ' he bawled to the frightened barmaid (the missus's daughter, by the way), 'bring me a -- bottle of -- whisky; and be -- quick about it! I come from BRICKVILLE.'

"When he had drunk the bottle of whisky in one long bubbling gulp, and when the drops had finished dropping from his awful beard, the barmaid, with some courage, managed to whisper, 'And when - when are you going back - to Brickville?'

"'Dammit!' said Angus, crashing the empty bottle to the floor, where it burst with an awful crash, 'I ain't going back; they've put me out because I'm a pansy!'"

Imagine the others! I substitute dashes for the "bloody" Roy used. Read back and try it!

So often talkative, cheery folks are content merely with charming. Roy was much more than that. He interested himself in our immediate future, and through his kindly offices we were given the use of a furnished shack on Magnetic Island. The result was that we spent but a few hours in Townsville the next morning, leaving for Magnetic Island at noon.

We had heard of Magnetic Island when farther south. I had imagined something a trifle fabulous, a sort of Gulliver's Travels island, or at least with some quality which put the compasses of ships out. It is, of course, a conventional enough island a few miles off the port of Townsville, quite subject to all the laws of Nature. It has nothing new to contribute to Bill's ideas of Nature. Nevertheless it is impossible to play too heavily on the words "attractive" and "drawing" when thinking of Magnetic Island. During five weeks, from the day we left Sydney in mid-winter, we had travelled in radiant sunshine. Nights were cool; sometimes they were even very cold; but every day was a beautiful day. Somehow Magnetic Island made a summary (a ghastly chance for a pun which I avoid) of all the kindly warmth and balmy air we had enjoyed. It was never unpleasantly hot. We rested.

Our little shack looked across the Great Barrier lagoon. Below us was a small bay of soft white sand always filled with radiantly blue water which was just pleasantly warm. Sharks never entered it. I don't blame the sharks; had we depended on fish from that little bay, we should have starved. Dick and I used to sit in it for hours, but we caught only three little fish in it during a week. Dick had, however, good sport trying to shoot immense stingrays and turtle off the outer rocks of the island; and, generally, we had a great time rambling and exploring. I worked most mornings, writing the articles (which never sold); Dick was supposed to fish for the pot. Except for coconuts, there was little fruit at Arcadia (the district of Magnetic Island we lived in) and Dick one day decided to cross the island overland to a pineapple and paw-paw farm. He was soon "bushed," and spent much of his day trying to get back. He met a tiger snake sunning itself on a boulder; and the snake instantly made for him. He blazed off his Mauser, which makes a report like a field howitzer, and exit snake! He wrote to his people in New Zealand about this awful encounter, and they shuddered.

Magnetic Island seems to be composed of sandstone boulders which have been shaped into all kinds of mushroom formations by weather. It carries in decorative quantities the pine known as the Norfolk Island pine. The inhabitants are engaged in fruit-farming, chiefly for the local Townsville market, but the island is largely given up to the entertainment of tourists and trippers. There would seem to be four settlements, named (charmingly) Nelly Bay, Emily Bay, Mandalay, and Arcadia. The boarding-establishment at Arcadia is extraordinarily beautiful - one great exotically painted dining-hall with thatched roof and open sides and a few reception rooms in a veritable bower of lovely ferns, multi-coloured tropical plants, and tropical 'flowers. Guests apparently live in small detached rooms surrounding the main building. We had our private shack, and were, I thought, too obviously unpopular with the boarding-house folks. We had tea there once or twice, and I cannot say I was agreeably impressed with the gracious conduct of the Arcadians. They were not actively objectionable, but I decided that a perusal of Henry Ford's book and a consequent understanding of "service" might have done. them good. It is really so easy to smile; the guests did the smiling at Arcadia! At this second, with the glorious vision of that lovely isle still fresh in my mind, I still feel that, if the waitress had returned our smiles with a pleasant little nod when we paid her, if the man on the place had attempted a "Good day" occasionally, and if the men on the fine launch which carried us to Magnetic Island had broken into a cheery grin once or twice, my memories of Arcadia would be even more delightful.

We carried guns with us. After we had landed, a very acidy gentleman approached with a scowl and said, "A game ranger came down on the boat with you! Hide your guns!"

No game ranger had travelled on the vessel.

The gentleman was telling us that Magnetic Island is a game sanctuary. Surely it would have been just as easy for him to have asked us if we knew shooting was prohibited. Dick and I would never dream of killing protected game-if there were the slightest chance of being discovered!

We spent upwards of a week on Magnetic Island and returned to Townsville late one afternoon. We had asked the garage folks who were overhauling our car to find us a camping-place during our absence; but the best they could offer was a place called Kissing Point. That sounded much too obvious; time was flying and darkness was approaching; we therefore decided to break a rule and to put up at a local hotel.

By a very happy chance *The Mikado* was being produced at the local theatre, and we went. I have been in many beautiful theatres, but I recall none with quite the charm of the tropical theatre at Townsville. It was called, if I remember rightly, The Winter Garden, a quaint name for a theatre in a place where winter is unknown. *The Mikado* was adequately produced, but with, naturally, a rather thin chorus ; and the fine voices of the principals lost much in what practically amounted to open air. Nevertheless, *"Oh, pray make no mistake, we are not shy-we're very wide awake, the moon and I,"* reached us beautifully, and became something of a slogan during our trip. Whenever we were descending almost upright slopes into river-beds and creeks, one of us working a rope and tackle while the car shuddered and shook her delicate way down, we would invariably sing, *"Oh, pray make no mistake, we are not shy--"* Presumably because we were - very, or terrified, with death and destruction sometimes not far off.

Another song that we found useful was less classical, but we thought the melody charming -"There must be a silver lining a-shining for we." This was useful when water and food were scarce, when camping-grounds were elusive, or when some river-bed seemed impossible. We had to make the last word plural, and unfortunately nominative, because, like "me," the correct word, it rhymed better with "sympathy" than "us." Or doesn't it? Those who know, or knew (for it is now antique), the song, will understand what I mean.

Townsville is a fine town. I am not sure that its main street cannot rank with the beautiful streets of the world. Along its centre are long narrow islands always alight with brilliant crotans, coleas, and other highly-coloured tropical plants. Palms are everywhere. We met few people, and I can therefore give but the poorest impression of Townsville. The mayor was courteous to us ; the owner of the garage where our car was overhauled did his best for us ; and two enthusiastic owners of cars like ours were pleased to see us and very indignant with the local motor world. "If you try to buy one of these cars," they said, "you've got to vamp the car agent and override all his objections. It's because they're bad for trade - don't use enough petrol, and seldom require repairs." That should make exciting reading for the people who supplied us with our car; but, not being concerned with advertising, I must hasten to add that I think the gentleman had made a mistake. Our little car proved herself the best of her kind in Australia over the roughest and most impossible kind of country. She was magnificent on good roads and brave on very bad; but, being a miniature car, the fact remains that she cannot "track." Therefore, on an indifferent road with deep tracks cut by the standard size car, speed was impossible, and driving not very comfortable. The roads in the neighbourhood of Townsville are execrable; no car makes easy way; but a modicum of comfort can be enjoyed by keeping in the tracks of other cars. Our baby - and how I would like to lie for her, bless her! - had a very serious struggle. When the Queensland roads are improved even a little, agents will be fighting for the privilege to sell cars like ours.

The agent we met was extremely patriotic. He had started business selling only British cars, but he could not make a living. " You can't live," he said, "on flag-wagging, no matter how much you may want to.

"The British car-manufacturers do not study Australian conditions," he added; "the Americans do."

I have heard that so often in Australia and New Zealand that I feel impelled to protest. American manufacturers do not study Australian conditions. They study conditions in America, where nearly all their cars are sold. Except for the great highways in the States, which in the eastern part" are nothing to write home about, American roads are often very bad. They are bad because the great extremes of heat and cold of a continental climate make road-building very difficult, and a temperature in January below zero, followed by intense tropical heat in August, will play the devil with the most carefully built road. That fact is taken into consideration by the Americans. The car sold in the States with the smallest profit on each individual car but with a mighty turnover can be sold in Australia cheaply. American and Australian road conditions are very much the same. British and continental roads are good - very good. The British manufacturer naturally makes his car to suit. the conditions found where the greatest number of his buyers live. He does try to meet Australian conditions, but it is harder for him, and very expensive. Nevertheless, given the choice of all cars, I would choose without hesitation a British car; and more particularly would I choose a British car if I were embarking on an adventurous journey which would take me hundreds of miles from spare parts. Every item of our little car proved completely reliable. If one part, even a part valued at less than a shilling, had failed, we could not have reached our destination. However, I hereby promise never to become serious again. I am hopelessly biased in regard to British goods; our life as a great Empire depends upon their success. Nevertheless, I should not travel on a British roller skate if I thought an American or a German one better. But there you are - I could never think that. And (may I whisper) I don't believe an American could either! I have lived in the States and know many Americans; they have excessively good taste. "Domestic or imported?" often asks the assistant in a New York store. "Imported, please," replies the customer, if his bank balance is good. The amusing part about that is that sometimes the domestic article is better! British workmanship has a glorious reputation in the foreign world, and deservedly.

    The coast road from Townsville to Cairns literally defies description. If you find yourself on a respectable piece of road, you may be quite certain you are not on the main north road. You have taken a wrong turning - very easy to do, for the main highway passes stealthily through forests and over creeks and rivers, many without bridges, and is often hardly more than a miserable track. It is now necessary to ask directions, if it is possible to find anyone to ask. The difficulty, notably between Ingham and Innisfail, is to find an English speaker. When we left Ingham - a deliciously exotic community of prosperous sugar-farming brunettes - we found ourselves rushing some miles along a tarred road. I knew we were off the main highway, and said so.

"Oh, go to Halifax!" said Dick rudely, jamming his foot on the accelerator and making the Baby fly - at forty-five miles an hour.

I was perfectly silent after that, but I must confess to some joy when the innkeeper at the townlet we eventually ran into said, when asked the name of his place -" Halifax!"

We retraced our way, chose the foulest-looking turn-off going northward, but were compelled to pause at forked roads. Tully was our immediate objective, so we motored along the road a few chains to where two dark men were standing near a sugar farmhouse.

"Are we on the road to Tully?" I asked politely.

They both smiled sweetly and showed beautiful white teeth. I smiled back and repeated my question.

The only result was a sequence of noises which sounded like the conjugation of a Latin verb.

I shouted gaily-"Tully-Tully-Tully! The way to--? *La rue* - towards?"

The brunettes instantly went through the declension of a Latin noun - and smartly!

I then pointed towards the forked roads and again shouted, "Tully-Tully-Tully!"

The Italians were delighted and crowed with joy. "Yessir-yessir!" they yelled.

"Oh, but which? " I pleaded.

"They mean that both go to Tully," said Dick reasonably. "Better ask them which is the worst, and then we can take it; because it will surely be better than the bad-- "

I stared at him malevolently and began again: "Dammit!"- very effective; they stood at attention! - "which road is the good road to Tully - *la direction a Tully - the rue -* the direction?"

I paused. The two men were standing staring at me. I think they were now a little frightened. I know no Italian; but it was most important to drag information from them. At last I whispered hoarsely- " Which- which is the *via dolorosa* - the *via dolorosa* to Tully? "

But this grand inspiration had the poorest reward. The two men groaned as if in pain; they made guttural sounds and finally produced: "We no spikky te Eengleesh!" Thereupon they turned on their heels and ran quickly into the farmhouse, where I am certain they burst into tears.

In the *towns* of this area of northern Queensland where Italians are in great numbers the matter is simpler: Chinamen or blondes are chosen.

The Italians are making great headway north and south of Innisfail, where actually is found the very best land on the Queensland coast. They are thrifty and industrious; therefore they succeed. I have heard people say that if Anglo-Saxons were equally thrifty and industrious they would be equally successful. I do not think Anglo-Saxons can be. The Italian has, surely, more red pigment in his skin; he can labour more successfully in powerful sunshine. Nevertheless British Australians do very well south of Townsville on the sugar lands, and they never appear jaded or seriously anaemic. "We were told that all this fine land was originally farmed by Australians, who accepted immense prices from Italians for their holdings. The Australians, it was said, now live in the towns in pleasant comfort.

It would be untrue to say that during our journey from Sydney to Townsville we found any farming families, dairy or sugar, living what I should call comfortably. Conditions often seemed bad. The older folks seemed happy enough, even in small bark humpies, but the great contrast which must be offered to their children when they visit their town relations with smaller incomes cannot encourage them to remain on the land. There is romance in thick delf cups and saucers, even in an earthen floor - the warm shadows of the rich brown bark walls of a humpy, often its quaint proportions and the smoke-stained furniture, are attractive - but a fine big bungalow with modern improvements and a splendid garden with even a tennis-court are quite within the reach of most farming families, and surely better! I love Australia and Australians as well as my own country and countrymen of New Zealand; but a farmhouse in New Zealand is a palace compared with one in Australia. We were, of course, never far inland enough to meet "sheep" folks; they, I am often told, "have butlers!" That sounds very impressive. But the children we met on the journey - beautiful kiddies! - in the farming areas were not, I am convinced, surrounded by enough of the grace of life. One other point, and then I have finished with criticism. I noticed more than once that very respectable fathers made no objection to their small sons being present when they yarned in the evenings. We all know the kind of stories that are exchanged when even decent men get together; it all seems natural enough (as Roy's mate would say); but I wonder if it is really good, from a moral as well as from a biological point of view, to soil small minds too soon or even to stimulate small bodies years before normal maturity. I hope I may be forgiven for saying this: upon two occasions I was present when very uncertain stories were being exchanged, and when two fine little laddies were listening with their ears very wide open and their eyes shining. One small boy offered a story himself; it had great success, even with his father, whom I know to be a highly respected citizen. When Labour in Australia gives up the futile practice of trying to put new wine into old bottles with useless strikes and lockouts and concentrates about seventy-five per cent. of its effort on its children, fighting to get everything good for them, it will enjoy unlimited success, and no one will have anything to fear.

The best answer to my criticism of rural living conditions is, of course, that, except for a very few weeks in the year, houses, notably in Queensland, are almost unnecessary. In that land of sunshine - and Australia, all of it, seems a land of good sunshine - why worry about a house?

What wonderful days we enjoyed! It became a great joke each morning as we emerged from our tent for one of us to remark as he glanced at the cloudless sky, " Well, I almost think it might be a good day to-day !"

And fruit! Never in my life, except perhaps once on Norfolk Island and again in Portugal, have I tasted oranges like the Queensland species. They have thin skins easily removed, pips do not worry; you simply drive a hole in one end and straightway enter a gourmet's heaven, which is a very nice heaven indeed. We ate at least a dozen a day each. We thought the Cardwell (just north of Ingham) oranges the best, but this may have been owing to the charm of the orange orchard's owner. She was a widow, I think over forty; but she had the jolliest of round faces, shining with a personality which was wholly kind and cheery. She must have been a marvellous flapper thirty years ago! She refused payment for the sugar-bag of oranges we had meant to buy, and so we suggested a joy-ride, wanting her to start off at once.

"Not in these!" she laughed, glancing at her working dress; "I'd be sure to meet someone."

Within the twinkling of an eye she had flung a fresh little frock over her head. (I saw much of the process through the French windows 'of her house!) On her neat head dropped a smart little pot-like hat, and she was off along the road with Dick looking very nippy indeed.

While she was away, I discussed orange-growing with her son, a fine handsome young fellow of about twenty. He said the quantity of oranges the orchard could produce was unlimited, and they were always good in Cardwell; but it was hopeless to bother much about them when the labour law commanded an orange farmer to pay a pound a day to pickers. I understand that the law has now been repealed. Therefore I hope the widow has now sold her motor-truck, which kept the wolf from the door, and that she is again concentrating on her oranges to her own advantage and the great advantage of the lucky folks who eat them.

Of course, while we enjoyed this glorious journey, through days and days of radiant sunshine - not yet unpleasantly hot - our content was not shared by the men who occasionally sat around our camp-fire at night-time.

"See that great black cloud coming over the mountain?" said a rather thin, worried-looking owner of a great thirsty banana plantation one night; "it's rain. My God, *it's rain!*" Which may sound irreverent; but how fervently the poor fellow was praying for rain, with a grand place and, I suspect, a grand mortgage; and a wife and children!

"It's rain!" he repeated, rather like a starving man outside a barred bakery window exuding the scent of fresh bread.

"Ay," said his mate, critically examining the cloud, which certainly seemed heavy with moisture "we'll get ten inches to-night, likely!"

"This place will be awash within an hour or two," said" the farmer hysterically; "like it was last year at this time-creeks rushing, and, where we're sitting now, a lake a couple of feet deep. Our bananas will be saved - !"

I glanced at our little car and camp and shivered, trying, oh, so bravely, to hope he was right. Obviously our prospective purchaser on Thursday Island would not drive a handsome little car if it floated away with the debris of a flood.

"But look here, old trout," said Dick, " if you can swim, we can't! "

The farmer glanced at him bitterly. He laughed hollowly. He bent towards Dick and whispered hoarsely, "It won't rain - it can't rain - it--"

"Ain't gonna rain no more, no more," broke in the mate, and we all laughed. It is quite impossible to imagine an Australian not laughing - even with his hangman!

But it seemed less amusing the following morning, when, in radiant sunshine and beneath a cloudless sky, we inspected the vast banana plantation with its bunches of hungry, starved fruit, and when we sensed a desperate situation, and perhaps ruin not far off. Indeed, with our tent packed up and the car ready for the road and higher land ahead of us, we hoped the good fellows would get all the rain they needed, and said so with complete sincerity. It would not then have mattered to us if the road did become a quagmire!

Part of the author's film of this event can be located on the National Film & Sound Archive's website.

3

In and Around Cairns

WE had been warned very sternly by the secretary of the Automobile Club in Brisbane not to attempt the Townsville-Cairns coast road. We would have followed his advice, but the inland way added some hundreds of miles to our journey, and our experience of an inland road from Brisbane to Rockhampton had not been very exciting. It had meant simply a drive through an endless eucalyptus forest, emerging occasionally at small towns and settlements. Of course the inland road is generally better than the coast horror, and it will " get you there" more comfortably; but we wanted to see men and things, and the coast road seemed more populous. We both love the sea, being islanders; and we dislike being too far away from it. Therefore we had tackled the coast road, despite the fact that few, if any, cars ever go right through.

We had left Tully one Sunday afternoon and were negotiating the Tam O' Shanter Range with some difficulty. Although most of Queensland seems to be baked up during nine months of the year, the area south of Cairns and around Innisfail has a copious rainfall during all seasons. Therefore we were enduring a most unusual experience: the road was actually slightly damp, and the creeks were running. Moreover we were passing through what amounted to true tropical forest - not a gum-tree within sight, nothing but tall luxuriant trees standing up high and bravely beneath a terrific weight of rich parasitic vines, mighty clumps of ferns and pendant orchids. Near the top of the range-I think we were beginning to descend - a charming creek of spark¬ling water crossed the road. Dick was driving; I had learnt to drive, by the way, and took my turn when permitted-which was not often! He paused. "Oh give it a burl; she's not deep! " I urged.

Unfortunately she was - very; the car just managed to get her front wheels on the far bank before the engine gave out. Water entering the radiator was caught by the fan and efficiently sprayed over the engine and notably over the magneto. We pushed the car a few yards along the road and made every effort to force the engine to go. If every turn of that crank handle had been the hour hand of a clock, we should have been there a hundred years, or more. We dried out the cylinders again and again; we worked on the magneto;

the carburettor was removed and taken down three times. The engine had definitely decided not to go. We had naturally no idea that our Baby wanted a little music, otherwise I would have sung to her. I hesitate to call her a little rat; but within an hour she was behaving like one, following an Australian Pied Piper (or fiddler) of Innisfail.

While Dick had his head buried in the bonnet, I boiled the billy; and when the eggs were cooked and the brown bread and butter spread out on the niece's tablecloth with the red, blue, and yellow border, now badly tea-stained by the sister's Doulton teapot with the dribbling delivery, I called him to *kai*. By the time we had finished our meal it was quite dark. Despite the annoyance of a not unnaturally striking engine, the peace and beauty of that scene were encouraging. Our camp-fire was illuminating the rich glen - I recall the scene so easily - and the cruel little creek was making up for her deep wickedness by singing most musically.

We were smoking away in great content when we heard the sound of another car approaching down the road. Very soon great headlights shone on the water. The car had stopped. "It's deep!" I shouted. "That's all right," yelled a boy's soprano voice; "we're putting a sack in front of the radiator!" The car took the plunge safely and drew up alongside us.

I presume that a motor vehicle passes over the Tam O' Shanter Range road not more than once a month, if that; but the appearance of thiscarseemedperfectlynatural.

It contained two men and a boy. We offered them tea and explained our difficulty. They refused tea and offered sympathy, but no practical aid, which seemed unusual. " You should, " explained the boy severely, "have put a sack in front of your radiator; then you'd have been *quite* all right." Excellent advice, incidentally, when crossing running creeks.

Suddenly one of the men said, " Would you like my mate to play you a tune on his fiddle? "

"It would be very nice," I replied.

"Go for it! " said Dick.

The Baby Austin said nothin'like the Tar Baby; although I must confess that I did hear a faint squeak, which I stupidly put down to contracting metal as the evening cooled.

The mate took out his violin, and, standing there in the glen with all kinds of shadows leaping around him as the fire blazed, he began playing old-fashioned little jigs and tunes. I think perhaps he played badly, a little scrapingly and squeakingly; but there were courage and verve in his execution with an effect wholly charming and stimulating. I know I felt impelled to execute a Highland fling over and around the camp-fire. The Baby, meanwhile, was making all kinds of metallic little sounds; which, again, I put down to contracting metal.

When the fiddler had been playing for about ten minutes, he returned his violin to the car.

Both men said "good night," and their car passed into the night. Hardly aware of what I was doing, I cranked our car, and her engine instantly began after the first turn. Within a short time she was following that fiddler.

The fiddler told us he was a plumber in Innisfail; but it's not only bathroom pipes he deals with. Pan-pipes are more in his line!

I have another incident to relate of our Baby's humanity, but it must appear in its proper place. I may add here, however, that I believe she knew she belonged to us. We sold her twice. She always commanded a good price, too, but by devious ways - even through a hurricane which should have wrecked the ship upon whose decks she stood, and a disabled ship at that, with a smashed propeller - she came back to us. And she only left us when, perhaps, it was best for her to go. She was a little too old and worn to carry us all the way round the world - a journey we began in her soon after the Cape York adventure - and therefore sank to the bottom of the Pacific in the hold of the R.M.S. *Tahiti* gladly enough, knowing she was adequately insured, and that her work could be done by a much younger sister. Still, she took something of my heart with her and, I suspect, something of the hearts of many Australians who read of her end and who wrote to sympathize. Her end was magnificent, and terrible. I can still see the great ship flinging her beautiful bows upright and majestically dropping beneath the waves; and I can still imagine our little car straining at the ropes which lashed her to the iron decking of the vessel's hold as she sank. But, of course, that is another story; we must now carry on with her really delightful adventure.

The road became worse and worse; the rivers and creeks, all running, became deeper; between Innisfail and Babinda it was really out of the question. But we struggled on, and after Babinda there was a great improvement. It is impossible to blame the Queensland folks for the bad roads. In most lands they get a certain amount of rain throughout the year, but in Queensland it all comes at once, during a short period. The land is not adequately furnished with natural drains, and when the clouds burst, which they do, every creek becomes an invincible torrent. I doubt if any bridge made by man would stand the strain of the rushing water and the mighty boulders and rocks, to say nothing of the gigantic uprooted trees, which are carried by it.

After the very trying journey between Innisfail and Babinda we felt a trifle fatigued in the latter town, and the Baby seemed to think an evening pot of ale would not hurt her fathers. I noticed that she was making for the Babinda Hotel. But while she could lead us to a beer pump, she could not make us drink, because one shilling represented our total cash. An adequate cheque cashed in Townsville had run out in Innisfail in buying stores, and the bank there was closed when we passed through. A shilling, we decided, might buy two small pots, and we could easily have taken turns at a long one. But the hour being five-thirty, we knew precisely what would happen in the bar. Our little car would be seen; many good fellows would surely gather round: "Where y're going ? - Cape York? Gosh!" (or to that effect). "Come and have a drink!" And we all know what that means!

However, the temptation was too great; we dashed up to the hotel door, hopped from the car, entered the bar, and tendering our shilling as obviously as possible, demanded two pots of port-a-gaff. We drank these quickly and rushed back to the car. But we could not get near it. Pedestrian traffic in Babinda was held up.

It was impossible to answer all the questions fired at us, and very difficult to refuse the kindly offers of hospitality; but one point became clear - no one believed we could get very far north of Cairns. At this point in our story a glance at the map on p 38 may be useful. Cairns is prominent; we were at that moment a little more than twenty miles south of it. Cooktown will be seen farther north, and the great peninsula stretching up beyond it. It seemed impossible to believe that we were reaching the end of the great northern coast road.

"Why," said one of our new friends; "you'll never get to Cooktown!"
"Never get to Cooktown! " I echoed. "Why not? "

"Because there's no road between Cairns and Cooktown, now. There used to be, forty years ago, in the old gold-rush days - over the mountains - but slips and weather have destroyed it."

"One car, I believe," offered another man, "tried that road; he got twelve miles on the way - out of a hundred and fifty - and then his juice was used up - first-gear work, struggling through creeks and rivers!"

"And then, if you did get to Cooktown - and you *can't* - you'd never get any farther."

"Two blokes tried to walk it - right up to Thursday Island, " said a middle-aged man; "and they found their skeletons a year afterwards - killed by the blacks!"

"Anyway," they all urged; "it's thirsty work talking. Let's have a drink."

I glanced at Dick. I felt a desire, in the teeth of all this depressing information, to accept the invitation and to drink and drink - at these cheerful pessimists' expense; but the idea was wrecked in my mate's stern eye. He pays the most appalling attention to bar conventions. If a man buys you a drink, then you must stand him one, even if it's your last penny.

The scenery had changed considerably, notably to the westward, where it appeared grand, the tall bare mountains requiring only snow to give a definite touch of Switzerland. As we motored swiftly along the good road, I had a mad sensation as of going to St. Moritz or Davos for skating and tobogganing. Many people, I suspect, would decide that the mountains near Cairns were more reminiscent of the Scottish Highlands. Which may explain the name Cairns.

Apropos of Cairns as a name, it is amazing how trivial incidents and sounds are photographed and impressed on the mind when associated with a place. After we left Babinda that evening we paused beside some men unloading a railway truck near the way. We asked if the road remained good all the way through to Cairns; and from that little group emerged a very comely fair face, which said, "Yes, it's guid a' the way to 'Care-uns." It takes a Scotsman to give Cairns the music in its name. Months afterwards I mentioned something to Dick about these men unloading the truck, and he instantly replied, "Where we saw that cheery Scotch bird?" The Scotch bird had made but one chirrup, but there was light in, or on, him. Mackay, a town on the coast farther south, suffers more than Cairns; after all, we must

REFERENCE

1. The Matron and the Constable.
2. Over "the Bump".
3. The Crater Lake.
4. "Ole Bill" and the Baby.
5. "The House Beautiful".
6. "Cooktown Crossing."
7. Where the rope broke.
8. Byerstown Range Steep and Rough.
9. Surprising an Earl.
10. The Maori Mere.
11. The first car to reach Cooktown overland.
12. Ants that work by Compass.
13. Pigs, Snakes, and Gators.
14. Game Country.
15. First running water since Mitchell River.
16. Devil Devil Country.
17. Black Gins and Green Ants.
18. "Lonely Harbour".
19. Pushing "the Pram".
20. Dying cheerfully.
21. Telegraph and Grass Tree.
22. The Devils Twins.
23. The "Terrible Archer"
24. Melon Holes.
25. Dodging the Fire Demon.
26. "The Flying Missionary".
27. Saved by a "Billy".
28. Quicksands in Batavia River.
29. Black Labour and Turkey Curry.
30. The bell rings for the final round.
31. The Last Hurdle.
32. Turkey Bush or Puncture Plain.
33. The Baby takes to the Water

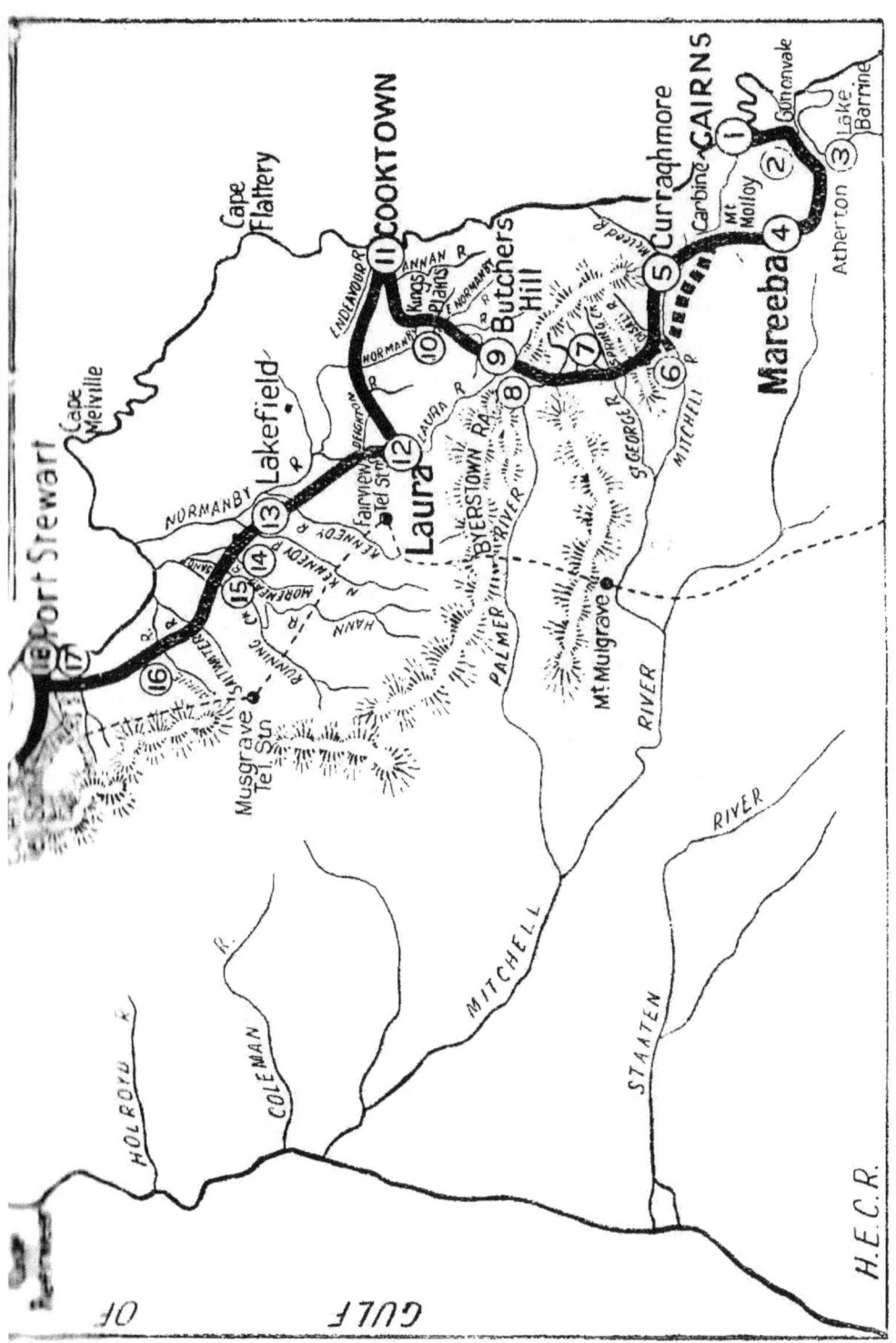

forgive the poor Sassenach, in that God made their tongues incapable of giving an "r" its full rights, And "Kens" for Cairns is not so bad; but when Mackay is rhymed with "bay" there is no excuse. Imagine talking of the "real Mackay" and rhyming it with "bay!"

Happily all the folks of Mackay, even the Greeks (and plenty of them there are, with their blonde waitresses) rhyme the name of their town with " pie." As they should!

It was too late to enter Cairns that night without looking like intrepid explorers. We still preferred to strike that nonchalant, " just going for a ride in the bus" kind of note, with the car and ourselves looking fresh and clean. I cannot explain this attitude. I dare say it was "drill" with me. Clean, smartly turned out soldiers have much more chance of getting there, than their dirty, untidy mates, even if it means fighting the filthiest kind of battle. I suspect we were slowly beginning to realize that soon we should be seriously up against things; possibly we were trying to deceive ourselves, and those we met, into the belief that a motor journey of more than three thousand miles, nearly a quarter of it over dangerous and roadless country, was really very little in our lives. Therefore we camped on the banks of the Mulgrave River below a great palpitating sugar-mill at Gordonvale. It was dusk, and we longed for a swim, but the long deep pools of the partially dry river could easily, we thought, shelter crocodiles; and we even feared to dip our billy in them for water. But the next morning, not long after dawn, we saw five or six very handsome flappers cleaving the great pool near the bridge; and so we joined them. They were vastly amused at our fears; but I wonder if the man who went for a swim in the fenced swimming-pool near Cairns not very long after is now amused, when he realizes that his other leg went to build up the tissue of an immense crocodile. One of the girls said, "Oh, if a ' gator' grabs you, all you've got to do is to bend round and stick your fingers in his eyes; he'll soon drop you!" My mother used to assure me that if a "black man" grabbed me in the street at night, he'd drop me at the first lamp-post; but I never believed her!

The holiday-like anticipation of Cairns is better than its realization. The great mountains are not far off, the lovely Atherton Tableland is near; but in Cairns they seem not of Cairns. The town has fine wide streets and good buildings, but it is impossible not to feel that its harbour is, or was, a mangrovy river-mouth, and that the town site was once an infertile mangrove swamp. The sea lapping the water-front appears stagnant, and is neither deep nor attractive; in fact it is rather cloudy.

Camping in or near Cairns promised to be difficult. Obviously, smart-looking fellows like Dick and me should put up at the best hotel; but it is difficult to escape under a pound a day at most northern hotels, and, since we proposed to wait in Cairns a week, this would have meant a good fourteen pounds. That we could not afford. And so we dug up the fierce man down in Sydney who had wagered us a hundred pounds that we would not camp all the way. That apocryphal gentleman was very useful! By a mere chance, we had chosen Shell benzine; we paid for our spirit, but the British Imperial Oil Company had shown great interest in our enterprise, and Shell officials were always helpful. Mr. Thorn, at Cairns, was particularly so. When he saw that we were determined to camp, he racked his brains trying to think of a suitable spot. Finally, he rushed us seven miles out of the city to the most seductive camping-spot I have ever seen - a shady dell near a deep, swift-running creek. But, with our car being overhauled in a local garage, it was difficult to see ourselves paying a visit to Cairns and dreaming on the pleasant banks of a river seven miles away.

And so we returned to the city. I felt certain there must be some amiable man with a large garden willing to take us in; but Mr. Thorn knew no one like that. He was living at an hotel and begged us to be his guests, which looked as if he had found us out; but I don't think he had. We continued rather aimlessly circumnavigating the city. Finally we found ourselves passing a large building on the waterfront with respectable grounds.

"What about that?" I suggested.

"The hospital!" said Mr. Thorn with a note of finality.

"Let's ask the matron; Dick might vamp her! " I said.

"Not before we've seen the secretary of the hospital board!" returned Mr. Thorn, showing himself a cautious citizen.

We ran this gentleman to earth at a tennis court. "In the matron's hands," said he. "Ask her; I have no objection."

"There you are," I teased Mr. Thorn; "we might have gone straight to the matron and - !"

"Yes, yes," said he with a very serious frown; "but you can't - you *can't -* !" What a little world of wheels within wheels Mr. Thorn showed with his slight emphasis and little frown. Well, he was quite right. It is a good rule for an aspiring young business man never to wound the amour-propre of a secretary, of any kind, notably the other sort, who have fat chiefs! You might as well brush out your throat with a hedgehog and pull him out by his tail!

Arrived at the front door of the hospital, we lost our nerve. There was a cold efficient business air about that vestibule which chilled us. We asked to see the matron, and were told to enter a small sitting-room; but we decided to let Mr. Thorn deal with the lady while Dick and I waited near the car. When we saw a white-robed figure fly over the top into his trench, we walked softly on to the veranda and listened to as much of the conversation as we could.

"Er-Matron," began Mr. Thorn charmingly, hiding his embarrassment very well; "there are two gentlemen from New Zealand-gentlemen from New Zealand!"

"And-- ? " said the sharp female voice of one evidently waiting to hear what diseases we had. In a second I knew the matron of the Cairns hospital had a million H.P. mind - speedy, but useless for towing.

"Well, these gentlemen -" Mr. Thorn was being very nice; but it did him no good.

"Yes - from New Zealand-go on!" we heard.

"They have - well, *they've a baby--* "

"What's the matter with it - not hook-worm - from New Zealand?"

"Yes," I decided; "I am right; the lady hates camouflage and adjectives! One must be clear and concise."

"I mean," went on Mr. Thorn soothingly (Quite useless, I knew. She's hardened to a bedside manner), "I mean they have a car, and they want- "

"Dear me!" said the matron, "two gentlemen from New Zealand with a baby and a car - ? "

"No, matron - not exactly; they-" But Mr. Thorn now spoke more softly, and we could not hear him; there merely followed the pleasant hum of his more gentle tones; and I really thought he'd achieved an alliance until I heard said in a kindly, exhausted sort of voice, but still very business-like: "What precisely *do* you want? "

I rushed to Mr. Thorn's aid then, and found in the small reception room a tall lady, into whose slightly cold eyes I smiled with a perfectly spontaneous desire to make a friend, because her head-dress was so immense, so soft and clean; because there was kindness and humour hidden behind the stern uncompromising demeanour she then wore; and because I knew she was efficient to her finger-tips. I worship nurses on sight, especially the public hospital kind with their grand background of discipline.

I made our request in a very few words, and got straight from the shoulder and tartly, too: "A most *unusual* request!"

Down I went instantly (and wisely); but I rose happily when, with a delicious wintry smile, she remarked: "But I don't see why it shouldn't be managed; where would you like to camp? "

We walked to the veranda, and the cool breeze from the lagoon caught the vast head-dress and snowy frock. For a few seconds I forgot all about camping-places.

"Where would you like to camp?" There was a slight return of the sharpness. I therefore dropped from Heaven (where the angels surely must wear big flowing head-dresses) to earth, and pointing towards some shady trees near two church-like little buildings, I said: "There, I should think - if you'll let us?"

"Two morgues!" said the matron; "you couldn't go there."

"But never used!" said Dick happily, with that sleepy, very reverent, gently manly line he uses on flappers from seventeen to seventy. "No one could possibly die here - not with -" And a gesture took in the hospital and the matron - but chiefly the matron!

I don't think Dick realized how narrowly he escaped suppression; he escaped, however.

"I think the doctor's veranda would be best - if he'll have you," said the matron; "I'll ask him." I believe she smiled a little when she turned her back. The great head-dress flying out as she marched along that cool passage had an unusual wiggle!

A few minutes later the matron returned with the house surgeon, and it was soon obvious that the doctor would take us in, and be glad to have us. I don't think he saw us as persons. He smelt Adventure. He led us to his veranda, and offered us more than one half of all he had.

He was young - twenty-four - and at that time I sensed a "give me a lovely island in the blue Pacific" complex, together with a feeling as of one wanting wide horizons - and Adventure. I saw that in his dark, eager, boyish eyes; and I felt it more strongly when, between intervals spent in looking after a small baby trying to collapse with hook-worm that night, he took out his violin and played to us. And he could play! That he envied us was obvious; that he realized the price one must pay for the privilege of roaming was not so obvious. By an amazing coincidence, and I think a lucky chance, I dropped a spanner in his gears, and, I hope, stopped him effectually from embarking on an adventure which would not have helped with his career.

Few people have been to the island which we had better call Koto. It is in the malarial area of the north-western South Pacific. It is an unlucky spot of land. One great historical figure saw his hopes wrecked there, and probably died there. An attempt to exploit the great natural resources of the island has meant the waste of many thousands of pounds, although that attempt still goes on and may end in success. I was in charge of the island and its surrounding group for some time, and, while I liked the place and my work, misfortune and great trouble followed. It would be untrue to say that my career was wrecked; indeed the pathetic effort to save a pair of wretched wild natives from the very silly arm of the law (quite successful, thank God!) which resulted in my leaving the place disheartened and distressed, actually saved me. While I was there, a very fine young medical officer came to look after the white workmen. His few months on the island nearly killed him physically; but in more serious ways Koto attempted to destroy him. A bad island, Koto; and yet a superbly beautiful place.

That first evening in the hospital our host showed me a telegram inviting him to leave forthwith - for Koto! "Hey," I said abruptly, "you're not going there - *you can't!*"

"Oh yes I am - as M.O.," said the doctor in some surprise. "Why not?"

I shook my head. "Oh," I repeated rather fatuously, "but you can't. Do you know anything about Koto? "

"Not a thing; I searched through the library and found one sentence. I was just going to send a reply to that telegram accepting the post when the matron came to tell me about you fellows."

"A miracle!" I exclaimed. "Do you realize that if you were to search the whole of Australia you could not find more than five or six men who know Koto? And I do - probably better than anybody on this continent."

The M.O. was amazed at the feeling I displayed, and instinctively reached to his waistcoat pocket for his thermometer; but I think I was successful. I gave him ten good reasons why he should not go, and, knowing that these would probably make him want to go, I added about sixty others, more subtle and less romantic. I think I won.

It was most interesting, being at the hospital and part of it, wandering hither and yon and fortunately not seeing much pain. Our host was deeply interested in X-ray photography, and one day showed us rather more than a thousand delightful photographs of fractured bones. We saw neat fractures, untidy fractures, splintered fractures, fractures freshly fractured, fractures coyly knitting, and old knitted fractures re-fractured. The M.D. dealt out the photographic plates like an immense pack of cards. Dick enjoyed it with the M.D., but later accused me of looking and being bored. Frankly, I was. I like a fracture well enough, but I feel that the mere operating-theatre photograph should be modernized. Why should not the newspaper reporter's little story of the accident be clipped out and photographed with the shadowy limb? Neatly placed in one corner it would supply articulation to the dry bones. In another corner might be added a snap of the bone's owner, to give the human touch and to add poignancy!

One morning the doctor said, "Come and see Claude," and we followed him to an outer ward in which lay a very respectable-looking inky-black aboriginal with a curiously well-trimmed moustache and nicely brushed hair. He reminded me forcibly of that nigger on the money-box grown old and more reserved.

Claude, who was of uncertain age, but fairly old, I guessed, seemed delighted to meet us, but more delighted to see the doctor, for whom he had plainly a fervent but slightly puzzled affection. I could see that he felt he was something of a trick to the doctor, and unworthy of it. Like all aboriginals, he had a goodly sense of humour, an ability to catch quickly the veriest shade of fun and not to miss his cue. He had been a tracker, concerned, it seemed, with the famous Kelly gang. He disposed of Ned in rather virtuous, and I think artificial, tones by remarking, "Me think he kill too many men!" One gathered that if Ned Kelly had murdered a mere two or three Claude would not have minded so much. But when he sensed that there was now no condemnation in our hearts for Ned Kelly, he added quite honestly, "Me think he pretty good feller - pretty good feller."

"How do you like Claude's moustache?" asked the M.O. suddenly.

"Very well," I said; "I'm particularly intrigued with the upward sweep at each end."

"I'm glad you like it," went on the doctor reminiscently; "I've done a lot for Claude operated successfully and luckily on him, cut off his whiskers, shaved him, and toned up his moustache. I was not quite certain about the moustache. Now that you agree, I'm glad I spared it. He looked like a baboon when he came here; he looks very nice now, doesn't he?"

Claude looked very nice-indeed, rather like the portrait of an early-Victorian great-uncle; but what looked nicer was the young doctor's sheer joy in his patient. Perhaps even nicer was Claude's quivering, humorous mouth and shining eyes.

"Now, Claude," said our host, walking to the head of the bed and looking affectionately down at the old man, "tell these gentlemen how you got speared; let them see the marks!"

Claude glanced at us shyly and apologetically as who should say, "Isn't he a delightful boy?" and dutifully drew back his bedclothes, exposing two old scars on his still magnificent torso.

"How old are you, Claude? " asked the doctor.

"Me no savvy, doctor; but me think me come a very long way, eh?" Claude shook his head a little over that "very long way," but soon recovered.

"Now tell us how you got speared!" Very tenderly the M.O. recovered Claude's great black chest with the light sheet. He then went to the window-sill and perched himself on it, waving one leg and watching Claude intently as he told his story. "Adventure!" thought I -

"Adventure! Not content with wanting to rush about Australia in a small car, he now feels he would like to have been Claude fifty-five years ago."

About fifty-five years ago Claude had killed a wallaby, and asked his brother to cook it while he sought another. Claude was unsuccessful and returned to share the cooked wallaby. His brother had eaten the lot. There was a fight. It seemed best not to inquire into Claude's late brother's fate!

"Don't mention Claude to me! " said a senior sister tartly that evening with a toss of her head-dress; "I've had quite enough of Claude."

"Rather a dear old chap, isn't he, sister? " I remarked.

"Listen!" she snapped; "I'd got to bed after a very heavy night. It was about seven-thirty in the morning. A message came from the house-surgeon. Would I go at once to number six ward to see Claude? I thought the old man was collapsing - he'd been very bad-' and I dressed and went. I could hardly drag my legs after me. It was to admire Claude's moustache that I was dragged out of bed!"

The sister looked very savage when she said this; but I must admit that she soon broke into a laugh, a cheery, happy laugh, like Claude's.

Legendary tracker Claude Ponto (far right) with his wife Minnie Connolly (far left) and their two children Teresa and Stanley, at Low Island near Port Douglas, Queensland, 1928 (courtesy Raelea Wangullay Connolly-Neal).

4

Dark Forbodings

AT the end, now, of the long road connecting the major towns of the eastern Australian coast, it was necessary to make final preparations for the difficult part of our journey. While the distance as the crow flies is much less, we decided to prepare for seven hundred miles. We hoped to find wagon roads occasionally, but nothing more than bridle-tracks and cattle-pads could be counted on. There would be several major rivers and many creeks to cross, all, of course, bridgeless. No petrol could be bought north of Cooktown. The Shell oil men had run to earth ten gallons at Merluna, roughly two-thirds of the way up the peninsula, and this was being kept for us by the cattle-station manager. We could carry four gallons in the tank, two on the running-board, and another eight on the back seat - fourteen gallons in all. On a respectable road that would take us easily six hundred miles; but cross-country work, we knew, would demand much low-gear work, and that is very extravagant. We might do twenty to the gallon; we might do ten; much depended upon the continued efficiency of the engine. We decided to abandon most of our baggage, and keep only what was necessary. We left Shakespeare and *Alice in Wonderland* with the M.O.; our tent and the suit-case, together with many another useful item, were packed ready for shipment to Thursday Island. Food was important, but water more so. I fear - and I realize now how shocking the confession is - we gave very little thought to food, and not nearly enough to water. We bound down the hood and covered it efficiently with its ordinary cover and some sacking. Dick very cleverly arranged an awning with stout linen held up by fencing-wire, and this proved much cooler and more useful than the ordinary black hood, which would have been unbearable, as events proved. Our object, as a matter of fact, was merely to protect the hood; our purchaser on Thursday Island would like a smart-looking hood, we decided. The car, in Cairns, looked perfectly fresh and new.

    With the idea of gaining police benevolence in the wild country, and the right to employ natives without too much red tape (the laws are very strict on that point), we called on the superintendent of police and showed him our letters of introduction. Our letters always proved useful. We had one from our own Prime Minister. He called us "reputable citizens of New Zealand" and left us at that. Another great minister of the crown - a personal friend - gave us one expressing what amounted to the hope that we should enjoy" the success we deserved!" Both ministers were badly licked at the next election, and we were not nearly so distressed as we might have been had they shown more enthusiasm. I do not think, however, that their defeat had a great deal to do with the letters. Sir Dudley de Chair, the governor of New South Wales, who was most kind to us in Sydney, sent us to the Premier. The result was something much more glowing, on good rich parchment paper with a great red seal near the bottom of the page. It recommended us to the whole world in fine generous terms.

 And so we placed the New South Wales letter on the top of the pile which we laid under the nose of the Cairns superintendent of police and watched him. He was manfully impressed, and, ringing for a constable, said to him, " Pitchem was in the Peninsula; take these gentlemen to him!"

 He then agreed to write us letters to his subordinates, and we followed the constable to the docks, where Constable Pitchem was on duty.

 I should point out here that the superintendent made no obvious attempt to advise us to abandon what he must have regarded as a mad scheme. He merely said, "Pitchem was in the Peninsula - take these gentlemen to him!" If the result was not what he expected, he cannot blame himself; he did his best!

 Constable Pitchem proved a fine-looking officer, given a trifle to *embonpoint* and beaming with good-nature and enthusiasm. By the way, the Queensland tropical and sub-tropical police wear khaki suits and soft hats turned up at the side. They instantly recall Boer War soldiers rather than veterans of the last one - perhaps they are a trifle too bulky for the last. The absence of the conventional copper uniform of navy blue and silver gives an initial, and wholly deceptive, friendly effect. That cold, arm-of-the-law, stern eye shines and freezes in Queensland, too.

 We told Constable Pitchem our story. We were going to motor to Cape York, and we said it without the slightest sign of the shuddering and shivering which had begun in our hearts at Babinda. He listened to us court-

courteously until we had finished. He glanced at the fat ship near us getting fed with an endless chain of sugar in neat little bags running across a bridge from the dock store. He gave something between a guffaw and a giggle, and looked quickly to see if we had joined him. We had not. The case was obviously desperate, and so he threw back his head, jammed one fist into the other, looked at me contemptuously and at Dick with pity, and said:

"Dammit - you can't!"

Then he took off his hat, mopped his brow with a handkerchief, looked at one of his stern-eyed mates, and said

"Dammit - they can't. Why- " But words failed him.

"Come, sergeant," I said gently, " and look at our car! "

Together we all rolled along the dock and through various storehouses to the main entrance, where the car was hidden, as one policeman said, behind a thistle.

Constable Pitchem stared at the car with great amusement. He laughed heartily and very boyishly.

"Dammit," said he-" I believe they can. *That* could! "

"Ah-- ! " I breathed.

"But," said he, crossing his legs and leaning against the shed with a stern, critical gaze on the poor little motor, "you'll have to sweep off the mudguards and-" He made a ghoulish gesture reducing our car to wheels and chassis.

I saw Dick and me nipping up Australia on a chicken-coop tied to an animated skeleton, without grace or dignity. I saw writ large on the sky, "Intrepid Explorers!" I sensed desperation, courage, and "round the world on a roller skate" sort of thing; and I said carelessly, " Oh no, she'll do as she is; at Cape York she'll look as she looks now."

That was not tactful of me; actually I was hardly talking to Constable Pitchem; I was thinking of what our bank balance would not be if the car were sacrificed on behalf of glory. I should have realized, as later I knew, that he could not regard the trail up the Peninsula as a boulevard.

It must have been excessively annoying to find two strangers telling him that they proposed to motor through country where he, on horseback, had suffered many privations - hard country, cruel, thirsty country, and half a thousand miles of it. And in the presence of his mates, *too*, who had often been thrilled by stories of his adventures "in the shocking north!" However, he was extremely nice to us, and invited us to call at his house that evening, to work out plans and routes.

We found him in the prettiest kind of house, with the most handsome and best kind of wife and a magnificent pair of thoroughbred Alsatians. We began by eating large juicy mandarins off a round table of Queensland oak. Most of the furniture was of silky oak, and highly polished with, I suspect, that compelling polish produced by elbow-grease. There were many lampshades of pale turquoise blue, and Constable Pitchem, his wife, and the Alsatians stood up to them very well. Only pleasantly furnished bones can. Our host now wore a soft white shirt, and the cold, arm-of-the-law eye was replaced by something boyish, cheery, and helpful. After all, it must be difficult to remain stern and uncompromising while your wife jeers at your figure. She had given her heart when Constable Pitchem was slim, it seemed; and I fear she has no chance of detaching it now that he is not. Which, of course, must be very awkward. A fine fellow, Constable Pitchem; we could hardly have done without him. And I say this with greater seriousness and sincerity than the tale of our adventures would suggest. We are very grateful to him.

Our maps were soon spread on the shining table, and a possible, but not very probable, route was worked out.

But what a way of horrors! At this moment I recall our host's serious face leaning across the shining table in that soft blue haze, telling us exactly what a Cape York Peninsula river could be. The rivers would be dry now, but a few thunderstorms would turn them into rushing torrents forty and fifty feet deep - sometimes more. There was what Constable Pitchem called "the terrible Archer," whose dry bed was filled with a mighty jumble of great round boulders fifteen feet and more in diameter. The river-banks were either precipitous or mere mountains of soft white sand.

Then there were wide areas of devil-devil country where the surface rises in a succession of sharp little hillocks two or three feet high, with sticks, twigs, and stout little stakes projecting from them - devil-devil country, maddening to horses and sometimes fatal to them.

"Boys," urged Constable Pitchem, placing two manly fists on the table and staring into our startled eyes, "if it rains when you're on devil-devil country - stop! Stop, I say!"

Our host paused and turned his eyes towards his knees. "If you don't stop," he said grimly - "you'll-you'll sink from sight!"

I heard the sough and gurgle as our car sunk in Australia, and I saw Dick's tow-coloured hair pause for a second, awash in the foul vivid mud before it too sunk from sight. Personally, I had managed to find a suitable branch of a tree from which I should later be rescued by kindly blacks.

Then Constable Pitchem told us of melon-hole country-great caverns in the clay surface disguised and hidden by tall grass, where horses broke their legs and collapsed in untidy messes, and there was no need to bury them! Sometimes the melon-holes had a thin crusty roof a few inches thick - and down you would go. The holes varied from one foot to ten feet in diameter, and often appeared close together, so that a way could not be found between them.

And food - and water; we should be scores of miles from help. At the very few cattle-stations, one or two in half a thousand miles, we should have to lay in stores amounting to hundreds of pounds of salt beef for ourselves and the natives whom we should have to recruit. (At this stage I wondered how a car weighing eight hundred-weight, already seriously over-laden with ourselves and the necessary stores and petrol, could add to its load hundreds of pounds of salt beef; but I let that go.)

"How long, sergeant," I asked weakly, " d'you think it will take us to reach Cape York? " I was counting on about three weeks, or at the most a month. At the end of a month, I had believed, we should be on our way to Singapore with the car happily and profitably sold and our bank balance in healthy condition. I admit that this optimistic view was becoming modified with all this devil-devil and melon-hole talk; but I was not prepared for Constable Pitchem's reply to my question.

"Nine months," he said briskly; "*about nine months.*"
"Oh, make it nine years, sergeant," I said bitterly; "you might just as well; we can't go."

Dick and I were greatly depressed. If we abandoned the enterprise now, at Cairns, the car would automatically cease to be ours, with consequent ruin; if we plunged blindly into the Cape York Peninsula with a nine months' journey before us, we could only call ourselves fools. It was then late in September; unless we reached Cape York before the middle of December we should never reach there. The rains begin in December, and the peninsula divides itself into a vast lake and a treacherous quagmire.

However, it was no good showing our feelings to Constable Pitchem and his wife. We sat in that pleasant blue haze and ate more mandarins, occasionally playing with the handsome Alsatians. And why not eat mandarins and play with Alsatians? All was lost. Our brave little expedition could only end dismally. For, if we escaped thirst, we should die of hunger; if we found food and drink, the devil-devil country would engulf us; escaping the devils, we should fall into melons; even if safe from all these horrors, how could we avoid the fangs of death-adders, brown snakes and tiger snakes, or even the teeth of mighty crocodiles?

We walked home to the hospital with an interval of one yard between us like a disillusioned married couple, a very bad sign, for Dick and I usually bump along together laughing over the day's joyous pantomime. Our morale was exceedingly low; for a long while we were silent. I felt more unhappy on Dick's behalf than on my own. Common sense warned me to take Constable Pitchem's advice seriously; but instinct, or something else, allowed me to take much of his depressing information with a grain of salt. While I knew Dick would never falter in the attempt, I also knew that he is guided in most things by common sense, much more than I am.

"Dammit!" I said at last; "we'll buy a pontoon and make the car work paddle wheels up the Great Barrier Lagoon from Cairns.

"Or look!" I continued; "we won't buy a pontoon; we'll plunge as far north as we can in comfort and then stop and say -"

"We'll motor through to Cape York," said Dick between his teeth; "we *will* motor through to Cape York!"

That did it; and I shivered. Pandora's box had not been shut in time - even hope had flown; for the last time that Dick used those tones we were motoring at forty miles an hour down the Ninety Mile Beach in New Zealand, with an incoming tide lashed forward by mighty rollers, trying to reach some rocks round which we must pass before the tide reached them, or else be compelled to spend a cold damp night on the sand. We had little chance; but, in reply to my doubt when the rocks appeared a few miles ahead, he had jammed his foot on the accelerator and had said fiercely, "We will get round the rocks!" Almost the next second saw the sand give way beneath us, as with a horrid shudder the car almost stood on her bonnet in quicksand, and we were gnawed in the teeth of disaster.

"Anyway," said I; "we can't go to the Barron Falls; we must start this business at once."

"Yes - no Barron Falls for us! "

The M.O. played us tunes on the veranda that night, and also saved the life of a half-caste Maori lady from New Zealand who had slipped on a date-stone. Together, the tunes on the violin and the story of the Maori lady's fall, saved us from suicides' graves!

The next day we were chatting with the local newspaper editor, a most charming and helpful man; but with Constable Pitchem's list of horrors in my mind I found some difficulty in giving him the sincere attention his words should have commanded.

Vaguely I heard: "Italians - yes - fine settlers - prudent and economical; but we must naturally have some fear lest fine Italians in few numbers become Mussolinis in bulk. We can," he was saying reasoningly (perhaps tactfully), "accept Mussolini's principles as fine and virile - sensible, if autocratic, when viewed from a distance. But there must be no cut-throatery-- "

I hope I am reporting him nicely; I admit detachment, with devils and melons in my brain; but I was instantly awake and alert when the editor stood up and remarked kindly: "Now we don't want any regrettable incidents in the Peninsula - be careful!"

"Yes, we know," I said humbly, "we know devil-devils and melon-holes and snakes - and thirst and hunger and - "

The editor stared at me. "Yes," he admitted, "these things are terrible, but they can be fought and overcome."

"But surely, sir, there's nothing else?"

"Oh, no," he replied dreamily, "simply the blacks!"

"The blacks! " I echoed -" but they're now pretty tame?"

"Oh yes, tame enough - but "- here the editor looked searchingly into my startled eyes, "take precautions with the blacks. Never let one walk behind you!"

"But why, sir?"

"It may never occur to that black," the gentleman continued without heeding me, "that black walking behind you, to chop off your head or even to plunge his spear between your ribs - *but it might!* "

The editor closed his eyes for a second, and looked dreamily. "There is," he said, "some strange instinct in the savage heart - to kill! That black may like and admire you; you may have fed and clothed him ; but he might also feel an irresistible urge *to chop off your head!* "

We smiled weakly into the eyes of that kind editor and rushed to the post-office, instantly dispatching an emotional wire to our friends preparing them for the worst .:

We spent the next day sorting our baggage, abandoning everything unnecessary, and by evening we were ready for a start the next morning. It was necessary to go south again for about twenty miles and then to climb up on to the Atherton Tableland. Then, turning north again, we should pass through Atherton town, through Mareeba, and on to Mt. Molloy. The road ended, we were told, in the vicinity of Mt. Molloy. From Mt. Molloy to Cooktown there was no communication by road. The distance was nearly a hundred and fifty miles, and no motor vehicle. had ever reached Cooktown by road. However, depression had gone; two days must pass before we should leave the road; it was going to be very interesting on the Atherton Tableland.

I admit we were quite vague about directions, depending wisely, I think, on local information. We cannot claim any credit for working out plans with care; we went lightly and cheerfully, did our best, and I think the Lord was with us.

Before leaving Cairns we made a presentation to the good matron. It was quite a nice little ceremony. I should add that I had spent some hours on my sister's Doulton teapot with the cherries and grapes painted on it, rubbing out all the tannin stains near the top of the spout with soft sand, and making it fresh and shining. When wrapped in pale blue tissue-paper, and with a small card attached, it looked very rich indeed. I formally presented this to the matron with a few well-chosen words, and she replied very happily. She would use it only upon special occasions when particularly nice friends came to tea. My sister, I may say, had used precisely those words when her church committee presented the teapot to her. But my sister had abandoned it when she found most of her best tray-cloths ruined with tea-stains. Perhaps the matron has a brother? But there, I cannot honestly remain under a cloud of ingratitude; we confessed that the teapot was a dud; I gave *Alice in Wonderland* formally to the M.O. - a copy I've read and re-read for many years. If it gives him as much comfort and joy as it had given me in very dark times, he will have much to be thankful for.

We left Cairns rather later than we had meant to, and the result was that we were forced to hurry in order to reach the bottom gates of the one-way Tableland road before they should close for the down session. It meant motoring to Gordonvale, thence by a branch road to the foot of the steep mountains, whence the most wonderful road in Australia begins an ascent of three thousand feet in twelve miles of exquisitely graded surface. We had some minutes to spare before the gates should close for an interval of three-and-a-half hours, and there had seemed no question when we were within a mile of them; but some very bad little boys placed upright nails on a bridge, and the nails effectively stopped us. However, the bridge was over a fine swimming-pool of good deep water, and the hours of waiting passed very pleasantly.

In concluding this chapter I must say that Roy's mate's slogan, "If it's natural, etc.," was constantly used by both of us now; and we had collected two more, even better in some ways. They were: "Am I a man, or am I a mouse?" and, "But now - ah, now, a wave of *virtue* is sweeping over him!" I might begin the next chapter by telling how we found them.

5

The Atherton Tableland

IT was in the lounge of a small-town hotel. An immense man, very much under the control of the local brand of gin-sling, was expressing himself. His intentions, like his humour, were amiable; but his affectionate and rather careless disposal of himself in and among the small groups of habitues, together with his war-cry - "*Am I a man?*" (shouted in a great booming voice), "*Or am I a mouse?*" (offered in the faintest whisper) eventually became boring, and it was soon the earnest desire of the early-middle-aged habitues, the good proprietress, the manager, the barmaids, and even the cooks and waiters to see the big man safely on his way home. While people persuaded in friendly tones, he remained amiable; when they were firm, he laughed at them; but when they grew impatient, angry, and even threatening, his mighty body, despite the annoying smile which invariably hovered round his admittedly humorous mouth, became a belligerent mass of muscle and sinew, instantly commanding respect! When his friends became really very angry and even abusive, he, still smiling, yet obviously ready to deal the king-hit (which would have been a truly awful blow) gave little nutshell personal histories of these early-middle-aged, rather plump, duck-clad gentlemen which never failed to provide smiles in others not immediately concerned - until their own turn came! He quaintly and mercilessly retailed his biographical notes, offering in precise tones just the kind of histories that plump, early-middle-aged gentlemen in ducks are apt to achieve in the tropics, winding up, or summarizing, with a delicious drooping at the corners of his mouth -"But now - ah, *now*: a wave of virtue is sweeping over *him!*" This remark, as I said, is in our collection.

When the five or six big cars in front of us during the procession up the Atherton Tableland one-way road slackened their speed to a crawl, forcing us to do likewise, we knew we were near the summit. They had been too quick and feared to reach the control gates before the fifty-five minutes allowed were up. I had better explain the Atherton bump.

The road is designed to maintain motor communication between Cairns and its neighbourhood and the great fertile. tableland. It climbs for upwards of three thousand feet in twelve or thirteen miles, has an excellent surface, a perfect grade, and allegedly a hundred and fifty startling, but perfect-

perfectly safe, hairpin bends. The road is often an efficiently designed cutting along the face of steep rocky mountains; but an error in driving could only be made once. I suspect that two cars might pass well enough, but the hairpin bends (and reckless drivers) being numerous, it is considered safe to maintain a regular programme whereby the road is open for up traffic for a time in the morning and closed during an interval to give down traffic a turn, and so on throughout the day and much of the night. Cars, whose numbers are taken at the bottom gate and telephoned through to the top gate, are ordered to travel at a speed not exceeding thirteen miles an hour; and because there is no way of making certain that this speed will not be exceeded, fifty-five minutes are insisted upon for the ascent, a heavy fine being rigorously inflicted if even a few minutes less are taken. A car driver is almost equally unpopular if he takes more time, and people in difficulty are ordered to run into sidings and, if necessary, await the next session. It is really quite pleasant to find motorists being forced to behave themselves!

We, having missed the one-thirty session, and it having proved quite useless to urge upon the gate-keeper that we, being so small, could hardly matter, were compelled to wait until six-thirty when a dozen other cars joined us. The result was that most of the wonderful ascent through magnificent scenery was made in the dark. Dick was driving, and enjoying himself. Had I been driving, I might have enjoyed myself too, but Dick would not have: it makes such a big difference on these occasions whether you or the other fellow has the wheel. But it was too dark; there were too many bends; as we climbed, the chasms below assumed the depths of Hades, and the road, actually adequate, seemed much too narrow to me. If Dick had had a paralytic stroke or apoplexy, nothing could have saved us. Meanwhile we were climbing, climbing, climbing, most often on second gear, but with an occasional hazard towards high; the powerful headlights of the great cars sweeping before us lit up the walls of the stern mountains, or made graceful hesitating curves of soft light over the yawning chasm below as they encircled bluffs, capes, and sharp promontories with too much searoom occasionally, I thought—a nautical allusion which might be pursued still farther by folks who dislike deep depths, high heights, and petrol effluvium combined!

Our arrival at the top gates created a sensation which we enjoyed immensely. While the cars ahead simply had their numbers checked and were allowed to go, the dim figure who read our number-plate growled something to another smaller figure which sounded like, "Well - here's your baby!" I saw two white hands stretch out towards the car and instantly a girlish voice excitedly yelled "Mummy - oh, mummy - here's the baby!" At once there debouched from the veranda of a house by the way a squad of at least a dozen lively figures, including something short and trim which I suspected might be the mummy.

"Oh, my goodness - what a pet!" said the mummy, and thereby summed up the family feeling just then. For she, the gate-keeper's wife, has thirteen children, many of whom were present and all of whom were trim. They collected cars like postage-stamps; we, as something rare in that region, were a great find - especially to the flapper, whose excitement and joy were understood and sometimes even excelled by the mummy, but not openly appreciated by the young men (I could just see neat profiles, hair parted at the side, and rather small muscular arms below the rolled-up sleeves of immaculately clean shirts) who thought all this joy and gush unnecessary, and said so - without any effect!

In the meantime we had taken out a powerful inspection lamp, and, while Dick explained things to the young men, I personally conducted a tour for the ladies. I noticed, but at first gave no significance to, the fact that the girl's head was always bent very close to any part of the car upon which the inspection lamp shone; indeed, I fear I was chiefly concerned in admiring the coronet of dark curly hair above the pale face with the fine features and large beautiful eyes. The mummy's brisk remarks and ingenuous enthusiasm were most entertaining, and I was considerably flattered that her charming daughter seemed perfectly content to be with me: it was not ever thus on our tour! And then the mummy said, "She's quite blind in the dark - that's why she needs that powerful little lamp! "I fear the adjectives of the ladies were rather limited -" dear" and " little "- and these were applied generously.

"Mummy, look at the dear little cylinders like cocoa-tins!"

"But, Nelly" - with a cunning chuckle, "look at the dear little magneto!"

"Oh - mummy - the seats and lamps and wheel and - isn't it a dear little car?"

"Yes," said the mummy apostrophizing the car, which with all this approbation had seemed to swell her little self up in that dim light. "You - you're a pet!"

"Are you referring to my boyfriend?" asked Dick severely, as he approached with the young men. The young men thought this remark a useful advance against feminine gush, but the mummy's eyes shone, and she nodded her neat little head and the girl laughed happily.

The daddy was not present; I think the family had an evening guest; for at one moment the mummy said, " Oh, my goodness! There's your father left with Uncle Egbert (someone like that, anyway) and me out here!" and, with one regretful glance at the car, she nipped across the road to the house, where she could be seen on a chair in the lighted room, listening courteously, with a most steady expression, occasionally relieved by an exciting glance towards the road. However, no serious guest could possibly hold her when it was suggested that she should have a short joy-ride; and, in reply to a shout from the daughter, she galloped from the house, and within the twinkling of an eye she was off along the road with Dick, shouting, "I'm eloping in a Baby Austin!" I remained to talk sensibly to the rest of this delightful family about oil-consumption, sparks, carburettors, and tyre treads, wondering if they guessed precisely how much I knew of such things. I don't suppose I should know these folks if I met them in daylight; but if they came within my ken in partial darkness 1 should sense them instantly by their spirit - rather an automobile kind of spirit, but a good one!

We motored some miles along a fair road and, following directions, turned off a few hundred yards and found a camp near the shores of Lake Barine. It was too dark to gain any impression of the lake; moreover it was also too dark, and we were too tired, to gather leaves and branches for our bed. We did not even boil the billy, contenting ourselves with raisins and chocolates, squatting within a ghost-like canopy formed by a great mosquito net, which now replaced the tent. It was a birthday, incidentally, and this may have inspired us to spend much of that night discussing past events in our lives and making little jokes, which became better and better as the hours passed.

In the morning we made an amazing discovery; Our bottle of brandy, held in reserve for accidents, was found empty, with the cork still in

The suggestion that a process of osmosis had gone on between ourselves and the bottle was abandoned as ridiculous, and we eventually decided to blame the Australian kangaroo, whose forefeet are notoriously sensitive and capable. We immediately went to the tea-kiosk near the lake to buy aspirins. I felt strangely ill; Dick was hardly in better case.

"Malaria!" I explained to the good lady who served us, "I shall be like this for the rest of the day: knocks one right out!"

I took three aspirins and felt rather worse.

"D'you think," said the good woman eyeing me gently, "that you should really attempt this wild trip over the Byerstown Range to Cooktown when you're subject to these attacks?" Her sympathy admittedly seared my conscience.

"Oh," said Dick, examining a fern very closely and slipping two white tablets into his mouth; "he only gets them once a year. Usually," he muttered, fortunately to the fern, "on his birthday."

"Well," said the lady counting out our change, " I do think you're both very foolish to make this attempt; we've heard you were coming, and all the bushmen say that it takes bush knowledge and experience even to get through on a horse from here to Cooktown, let-alone in a motor; and when you're not really strong--!"

"Pooh!" we said; "we're frightfully strong - really; but not today." And we were not.

This mysterious weakness perhaps spoilt our enjoyment of Lake Barine; but in a curious way it brought into sharp relief all the beauty of the crater lake and its reserve. Here, because of an equally distributed rainfall throughout the year, is found a very rich section of Queensland, where mighty trees which have grown easily can therefore offer soft timber, notably kauri, cedar, and that most lovely of all timbers, silky oak. Man, without a sharp axe, is shut out; for every avail¬able inch of space not forced to the accommodation of massive tree-trunks is taken up by shrubs, palms and ferns, and even the space above these, which might be expected to remain clear, is occupied by lawyer-canes with their beautiful palm-like fronds hiding the most deadly spears and hooks. Paths are cut near the lake, and one may therefore pierce to the heart of all this beauty without being torn to shreds. The lake itself is allegedly a crater; it is very deep, and is said to be delightful for swimming. And it is, as such; for the water is unlake-like in that it is not chilly: but frankly, while I enjoyed a dip, I had great distaste for swimming very far out, feeling myself to be poised on the vane of a very high steeple

The people at the tea-kiosk offered to take us round the lake in a launch and we gladly accepted. In my weak state following the malaria attack, I could not imagine anything more delightful than dreaming round the cool shore. But unfortunately the launch engine refused to budge, and my heart sank as a small oblong punt was brought alongside the jetty. Into this we stepped, and it instantly began to sink (for which I was thankful). Another, alas, was soon produced, and one of the officers in charge of the timber reserve prepared to row. The punt had a square bow; in fact it had two bows equally square, so that one might choose. It was designed for one person, or perhaps two, but not for two plus Dick; indeed, when he got in, the barge was well below her Plimsoll mark and, I thought, beyond the powers of any man to row for more than a few hundred yards. I had dark forebodings, and swallowed two more aspirins, hoping they would deaden all courteous impulses to take a spell at the oars.

As the morning progressed - and we were not early birds that day - it became very warm. We had not rowed far before beads of perspiration appeared on the oarsman's brow; soon his light shirt assumed map effects - those geographical pictures which form on wallpaper below a leaky roof - and two South Americas, remarkably alike, dangled on each side of his breast-bone. Possibly Australia was moistly outlined on his back, but I, being perched on the stern with the oarsman's feet pressed against mine, could not see that part of him. It was becoming increasingly obvious that he would need a spell; but the very thought of pulling that barge, which merely bubbled along during the oar stroke and stopped with a jerk at its end, exhausted me. Dick in the bows was in a state of coma, and lay like a log; no courteous enthusiasm to take a spell could be expected from his direction! I saw that we might easily be rowing that punt during the rest of the morning.

"Going right round?" I asked carelessly, observing sadly that the circumference of the lake was nearly three miles.

"Oh yes - might as well; we'd like you to see everything," said the oarsman, with an extra spurt which instantly formed two sets of Falkland Islands off his South Americas.

Of course there was much to admire. The different varieties of giant fig came very much into their own at the edge of Lake Barine. Here they could show precisely what wonderful things their species can do with roots. Roots, garnished with moss, small ferns, and lichen, dangled from branches in twisted cords; roots tied themselves into amazing knots; roots occasionally formed caves in which a goblin might live; and sometimes, with a wholly unusual impulse towards regularity and balance, roots in hundreds formed great pipe organs. The rich boughs of these trees stretched over the lake, sufficiently high to enable one to row beneath them - doubtless to see their roots. Many dark trees offered maroon and crimson blossoms; other soft delicate shrubs had leaves of palest yellow ; there were tree-ferns and lawyer-cane palms running amok; and altogether, what with the reflection of this riot of kindly colour on the smooth dark water, we were in Fairyland.

If only we had felt stronger I Dick remained like a log in the bows, occasionally opening a sleepy eye; I fermented in the stern, bubbling expressions of admiration and appreciation to the sweating oarsman. But this could not go on.

"Awfully decent of you to insist on doing all the work," I said, arranging my feet so that he could get a better lever weight; "but rowing's wonderful exercise, isn't it? "

Damn good!" said he with a series of spurts which instantly submerged all his maps in one ocean of perspiration.

I took the oars then, and cunningly got the barge's temporary bows round, rowing very slowly, very gracefully, and unobtrusively, back to the landing-place. Dick "fumbled" thrice. But my, "Oh not at all!" to his, " Let's take a spell, mate!" was quite adequate.

We had luncheon beneath a shelter with white-washed supports and beams, a place of rigid cleanliness, with pots of cool ferns about. We ate cold chicken with crisp lettuce and tomato salad and a mayonnaise dressing; moreover there were neat little scones, fresh from the oven, so light that each one had to have a penny placed on his top to keep him from floating away in the breeze. Immediately outside the dining shelter the mighty forest had been tidied up, but not unkindly disturbed, all rank undergrowth having been removed to allow only the choicest ferns and orchids to grow in sleek splendour. While we ate, a very solemn aboriginal sprayed this tidy area with a hose; but he had no tricks. In a small enclosure lived a tree-kangaroo, presumably a species of large opossum, but he was an unamiable beast and refused either to climb or to eat when urged. Noonday is the period of fast inertia to most of the local beasts - except green ants! They never rest, apparently, and are particularly vicious when you sit under their trees (*very* temporarily) for a mid-day meal.

While bidding us good-bye and accepting our thanks for her great kindness, our hostess again expressed concern. "I don't feel very happy about you," she said; "if one of those attacks comes on," and she eyed me with rather suspicious sympathy -"in the wilds - far from help really, you boys don't know what you are up against."

I feel now that I should talk heavily about the Atherton Tableland, its fertility, its wealth, and its possibilities to Queensland; but this I will not do. I know nothing about the Atherton Tableland, and yet I know just as much about it as most travellers know who pass quickly along its moderately well-kept roads between its well-cultivated pastures, enjoying its stimulating balmy air. But we found some difficulty in agreeing with the Mayor of Atherton town when he said, quoting from a speech he had made to a Governor General, "We are not now, your Excellency, in the tropics!" Frankly, we did not find Atherton precisely chilly, and, if it was not excessively hot, then it was definitely red, for an unusually long spell of dry weather had turned its haematite soil into fine dust which covered everything. It had even lightly dusted a vast four-decker wedding cake in a local confectioner's shop, and, when I said to the baker's lady serving me with wholemeal bread, "Is that cake simply for exhibition?" she replied, evidently dating me as early-Victorian: "Bless you, no! We have to pay wedding-cake decorators five-and-six an hour." Which left nothing more to be said.

During the process of buying a small Union Jack to fly on the car at Cape York, we asked for directions from the shopkeeper, who had, he said, plunged a little into the wild country separating the rich tableland from the cattle country round Cooktown. Said he:"You must get to the Cooktown Crossing *via* Mareeba and Mt. Molloy. The Cooktown Crossing is the ford across the Mitchell River, and is about a hundred and twenty-five miles from Cooktown. The road ends there; you cross the Mitchell; you see a big mountain on your right called Lighthouse - keep to the left of that. You have to cross the Palmer River."

We said we'd do all that, and left for Mareeba - not very much wiser!

We reached Mareeba late in the afternoon, and, desiring to shop here and hoping that we might gain useful information about the two hundred odd miles immediately before us, we found a good camp on the banks of a creek just north of the town. We had finished tea, and were smoking peacefully, when a rather stout, rosy-cheeked old-age pensioner with a delightful "ole Bill" walrus moustache approached and began staring speechlessly at our car.

"Is that," he whispered hoarsely, "a baby car? I mean, is it really a baby car?"

We admitted that it was sometimes called by that name.

"Has one ever been here before?"

"No, no," he broke in before we could answer, "I know one hasn't - except last night!"

The old man made the last remark in tones so mysterious and trembling, and he became so agitated, that I got up quickly to help him. But too late; with a muttered "My God!" he sat flat on the ground, with his fat legs forming the sides of a rather wide triangle and his eyes staring at our small motor. It took us some time to pacify him, but, when we succeeded, he became quite cheery again and explained his emotion.

"Last night," he said, " I couldn't sleep, somehow - not for a long time. Then I did. Then I was lying on the road, and something very small on wheels with a big hoot ran me down and broke all of my bones. When "they" (the old man didn't explain who "they" were, but we understood "they" were young and energetic with sharp noses and snapping eyes) "were gathering up all my bones, mending them quickly and putting them together again, I heard one say, "Poor old cove - why, he's been run down and all his bones broken by a baby car - such a little baby car to run down a big fat man and to break all his bones.'"

The old man went through that little story fifteen times, until Dick retreated under the car and I invented an engagement with a towel and a piece of soap at the creek; but some hours later we heard him paying a call on another old-age pensioner in a humpy near our camp. Midst the rustle of leaves in the trees above us, interrupted by the occasional tappings offered by Dick under the car with the inspection lamp, I could hear - A baby car - broke all the poor cove's bones ¬ such a little car to break all the bones of a big fat man." Indeed the following morning we heard it again, for during our progress along the main street of Mareeba, where cars of our species had never been seen, the old chap followed us at a short distance, collecting little groups, and I heard him once explaining to some very bored-looking gentlemen, "Such a little baby car to break a big fat man's bones - all his bones, poor old cove!"

In devil-devil country.

6

Getting Warmer

I FEEL that I ought to describe Atherton and Mareeba, the two main towns on the Atherton Tableland; but I know nothing about them. They are, of course, new towns, and at present seem to have each but one main street. A great future is assured to both. We shopped effectively in Mareeba, and the clerk who attended to us carefully wrapped up a tin of particularly nice biscuits. "As you pass through Palmerville," said he, "will you give this little package to my niece?"

We said that we would with great pleasure, remarking that the gentleman was showing great trust. "I know you'll deliver it," he replied; "and, if you miss Palmerville, eat them - the biscuits!"

"Oh no," we said, "if we miss Palmerville, we will post them to your niece from Cooktown."

"Thanks very much!" said he.

Constable Pitchem's route had shown a trail through to Wrotham Park and on past Palmerville to Maytown, thence to Laura; but no one seemed to know the way through to Wrotham Park, and so we decided to push northward as far as possible on roads, and then to trust to luck.

We left Mareeba towards noon and reached Mt. Molloy during the early hours of a Saturday afternoon. I must apologize for the paucity of my scenic descriptions; all I can offer is that, after Mareeba, we gradually left well-watered country, and before we reached Mt. Molloy we were again passing along a bush road between smallish eucalyptus-trees rising from parched, thirsty land. Ant-hills became more plentiful and seemed impressive; but they were insignificant compared with what we found farther north. The crossing of dry creeks was occasionally annoying; but other cars had passed, and we managed well enough.

At Mt. Molloy, I dug out the baker and bought an extra loaf of bread, fairly certain that before it became stale we should get more at Cooktown. But this was not the opinion of one of the bushmen I found talking to Dick near the hotel.

"Gad!" said he with a sarcastic laugh; "they're taking a loaf of bread - one loaf of bread! - to get 'em over the Byerstown." The Byerstown Range, it should be explained, runs between Cooktown and the country we were then in.

"But," I retorted with dignity; "we've got five pounds of flour in the tucker-box to make damper with." Had the man appeared more amiable, I should have told him that we had also a tin of prunes and a packet of raisins. He remained facetiously sarcastic.

"Look here," he said; "I've driven cattle over the Byerstown, and I know it. You can't do it in a car. You'll perish; you'll starve, and you'll break your necks getting down the river and creek-banks. And as for a loaf of bread and five pounds of flour - to take you over the Byerstown - oh, Lord!"

"I suppose," he added after a pause, " if you climb the North Pole in that animated bug-beetle of yours, you'll wear a wreath of roses!"

I was silent and disposed to be cross; Dick was smiling.

Look here," repeated the man, "give it up! Get back to Sydney and drink a quart of whisky neat - and dream it; dream it - don't think of doing it!"

Some hours later, we stood beneath the shade of a brilliantly red flamboyant tree talking to the manager of the Brooklyn state-owned cattle-station. He was considerably amazed when he heard of our scheme to cross the Byerstown Range, but he thought we might possibly succeed. He said, turning to us seriously, "Have either of you any bush knowledge? "

I was about to admit our total and complete innocence; but Dick quickly said " Yes!" He hadn't, of course; but the lie seemed true.

The manager continued. "It's not more than seventy miles over the actual Byerstown Range during that seventy miles there is only a cattle-pad - no road. When you get within fifty miles of Cooktown, at the Butcher's Hill cattle-station, you will find a bush road; it was used once by a motor-truck a year or two ago, and you should manage. There was once a good enough road over the Byerstown, but that was forty years ago; all the cuttings have been washed away, and fallen timber and ant-hills cover the rest. The old fords across the rivers and creeks do not now exist. I think you will have to allow at least ten days for the journey to Butcher's Hill."

The manager seemed to think we should have some difficulty in finding the cattle-pad near the Cooktown Crossing; drovers usually allow their beasts to "spread" some miles before reaching water to prevent the thirsty beasts from drowning each other in wild stampedes, thus making the trail indefinite for some distance; but, a mile or so on, it would become quite plain. He told us to steer for the right-hand side of a rounded hill that we would see on our right from the ford, and, giving us his blessing, he bade us good-bye.

Followed twenty miles along a very rough bush road, where the surrounding scrub, very stunted and ugly here, was literally alive with kangaroos and wallabies, and towards dusk we reached the once famous Cooktown Crossing. Years and years earlier, there had been two hotels here, the one on the south side of the river kept by Mrs. Riley and the other on the north owned by Mrs. Connolly. There had been stables and stores; the water of the Mitchell now running so merrily was cleaved daily, and many times during the day, by the brightly-painted red wheels of Cobb and Company's coaches carrying all kinds of eager folks to the Palmer gold-fields.

We were alone. Within a radius of more than twenty miles probably no other human being breathed. Glancing across the river, where the forest began, now without any break, we wondered at ourselves.

Our wonder, incidentally, was nothing compared to that of the wallabies and kangaroos, who stared at us with brilliant eyes while their sharp ears positively quivered.

At last we had reached the end of the road which began (for us) in Sydney, which had carried us thousands of miles without a break, but which was now broken.

I feel that I should do much more with that idea-the end of the road of thousands of miles; but nothing seems to come. I can only recall a parochial kind of interest in the Cooktown Crossing as a camping-place, and the chances of catching fish in the river. Dick shot a pair of fat little ground pigeons a few minutes before we reached the crossing, and these we ate with an appetite which thought only of the present.

The next day, being Sunday, we rested. Only once on our long journey had we broken that sensible divine commandment to rest one day in the seven; that was when we dived too enthusiastically into the creek on the Tam O' Shanter Range. We desired to avoid anything of the sort in future!

We spent hours lying on warm rounded stones in the bed of the Mitchell, allowing the cool water to wash away any thoughts of the difficulties confronting us. In the deep pools near us were many crocodiles (of that we were blissfully ignorant, even if they were of the harmless kind) and they doubtless cast many a dull ugly eye on the two white figures playing in the water like children. . The platypus, too, is found in the Mitchell, but he was characteristically shy. So were the fish. A crow, however, was not a bit shy;

while we were bathing he swooped down and stole the bullock's heart we had bought for bait in Mt. Molloy, leaving only a piece of blood-stained newspaper. Dick managed to catch a small cat-fish; we fried that with half a dozen eggs for our Sunday evening meal.

At dawn the next morning, with the car packed and safely across the river (fortunately unusually low), we were ready to start. We could see the round mountain or hill to our right, and, threading our way slowly through the forest along the river-bank we sought the cattle-pad which would lead us to Butcher's Hill. The going was not very easy; it was actually a matter of crossing many ditches and watercourses, between fallen timber and rocks and between growing trees. It must always be remembered that cross-country work in Australia, certainly near the coast, is a journey through forest. In fact most of our journey from Brisbane northwards was through the forest. It is seldom that a wide view can be enjoyed. Therefore, whenever directions are given, it must always be kept in mind that continuous forest, fortunately without dense undergrowth, will veil, and sometimes mask, the perspective. Again, I must point out that the pad we were seeking was made by droves of cattle coming from Cooktown's direction, seldom or never going. Cattle are driven south to Mareeba for slaughtering. Therefore the spreading I have mentioned was expected on the Cooktown side of the ford, and it was impossible to know which were pads made by local cattle and wild beasts going to water, or which would eventually join the main pad we sought. Always remember that almost the whole of our journey, from now on until we reach Cape York, is a trail through forest, surrounded by trees. I insist on that point because, whenever anyone gave us directions, I saw the place mentally as cleared country, like that of New Zealand; and I could never remove that idea from my mind.

On we went, very slowly, picking our way with great care, the engine working on extravagant low gear. We reached the rounded hill which had been to our right, and, passing it, we skirted its base and turned north on a faint cattle-track. I fear I cannot be very interesting here. I can only reach the annoying point that, after four or five hours' search, during which we often lost each other and once actually lost the car, we came to the conclusion that we could not find the cattle-pad, and that discretion pointed to a return. to Brooklyn cattle-station for better directions. We hoped we might be able to hire a native guide. The situation looked far from promising. If it took us one day to cover no miles, how many days would it take us to cover six hundred?

We returned to the Cooktown Crossing and made our way back to Brooklyn cattle-station. The manager, whom we had met a day or two earlier, had gone to Mt. Molloy to meet his wife; the station was left in the charge of Mr. Boland, a government officer looking over the station books.

" I've been expecting you all day," said Mr. Boland, and, when we smiled our humble appreciation of the gentleman's acumen, he added quickly, "Oh, not I! I know nothing or little of this country; it was merely that a couple of drovers, Brown and Pickering from Wrotham Park, stopped here this morning and said you'd never strike the pad - that we should see you back. They seemed so secure in this opinion that we kept dinner more than an hour for you!"

I glanced at Dick, now with his nose in a tall glass of lemonade. The sweeping bulge in his deck-chair lightly kissed the spotless veranda floor. From the corner of my eye I caught an occasional glimpse of the dining-room, in and out of which dashed a smart little body hastily laying a cloth and covering the table with food and crockery; and again I looked up into the slightly troubled eyes of the very tall elderly gentleman and said, "You're being very kind to us, aren't you?"

"I'm doing," he said evenly, " the very least I can do." His gaze wandered once more towards the crimson-roofed flamboyant tree outside the slip-rails of the homestead compound, where two days earlier we had stood in the violent heat asking directions from the manager. "If I'd known - if - "he continued, but in a flash I had read his thoughts, understanding now his enthusiasm to show us the utmost hospitality, an almost boyish enthusiasm which had in it a certain quality as of one making amends.

"The manager," I put in quietly; it was so important to lie; "asked us to come inside-to spend the night, or at least to take tea with him; but you see we were eager to get to Cooktown; we thought it would be so easy!"

At that moment I recalled our optimism and what it had met with on the other side of the Cooktown Crossing. We were wiser now, and a little depressed.

Still, we were not yet ready to say, "Thank God, we failed to strike the cattle-pad; thank God we lost the car - even thank God we had endured a little thirst!" We said and thought that a few days later; we both say it now with a

Crossing the Mitchell River.

Recrossing the Mitchell River after being bushed.

great wonder, for we know now that a far Greater Power than ours had ordered, "Thou shalt not !" And we obeyed, returning to Brooklyn with some hope of hiring a guide, not because we wanted to, but because we had to. We might quite easily have found the cattle-pad; actually it was often within a stone's throw of our wandering footsteps; but, had we found it and begun our journey over the Byerstown, the result might have been tragic. We had not enough water or good means of carrying it; we had not enough petrol; we had not even enough food. Of course I admit the absurdity of a couple of adventurers like Dick and me claiming Divine help: it simply seems fair, now that we are safe, to admit our debt. Even bad men pray in moments of trouble.

Our host seemed relieved. "Ah!" he said; " 'm glad to know you were asked to come inside - indeed very much relieved! I saw you go off"; again that troubled expression behind the shining spectacles, "and, well, y'know - bush hospitality! I had read of you in the papers, knew you were inexperienced - and some of these young fellows forget it was different in my time, very different."

We pointed out more clearly that the manager had not forgotten, and partially succeeded in composing our host's mind - but only partially; the fact that we had not been given beds or at least food when we first called at Brooklyn was bad to him, and no explanations could alter this fact. Hence he seemed totally unable to sit down, so eager was he to look after us; and he treated us with so respectful a courtesy that one became woefully conscious of worn stained khaki trousers and equally derelict shirts.

Glancing at my light canvas shoes and sockless ankles disapprovingly he said : "They're no good - not for the bush. If you put your foot on a snake, you're done. Plenty about, y' know, and in the dry creek-beds you'll strike small death-adders efficiently camouflaged. One bite on the ankle and - !"

I saw Dick grinning; I was therefore prepared and adequately defiant when he said, "He wears spats!"

"Spats!" said our host, unconsciously bridling, "spats - gaiter? You mean those things Mr. Bruce wears: dear me!"

Observing that my reputation was going down rapidly with one I desired to please, I ran out to the car and returned with a pair of leather-lined grey spats, smartly cut, actually bought in Piccadilly and last worn there, with neat little buttons complete. I put them on.

"Now," I said; "if a snake tries to bite me on the ankles - he can't. Moreover, I am saved from the discomfort of heavy boots - and what more can you want? I'll admit they look a bit funny in this rig-out."

"Spats for spiting snakes!" essayed Dick; "the spat comes into its own - a good scare headline for a newspaper, eh?"

But Mr. Boland was greatly amused and impressed. "A good idea!" he admitted; "a jolly good idea! Well, well! Who would have thought it? I wonder," he laughed, "if that's why Mr. Bruce wears 'em!"

I explained that the spats had been found beneath the torn lining of our kit-bag, that they had possibly been there for years, and that their discovery was really a god-send, since they were most useful and comfortable when reconnoitering tracks for the car through grass and stony country. By the way, most bushmen in Queensland wear light elastic-side boots, those horrors worn by our grandfathers and known in the army as Jemimas. They are sometimes worn by officers with undress blue. The Americans coyly call them Juliets. Being light and easily removed, they are very useful for bush-work in snake-ridden tropical country. So are spats. I tried to get Dick to photograph me in mine, but, while he had to admit their great use, and even forgave me, he disliked the thought of anyone else seeing them. Dick's sartorial development is late pre-wrist-watch. It would take a brave young man to wear spats in Sydney or Melbourne except at his wedding. And yet I always think well-cut spats finish off a man's appearance. I know an old pair of shoes, if well-brushed, regain life and smartness when gently covered by suitable spats; and bachelors with holes in their sock-heels can often thank them. 1 have - sometimes, but not in Australia!

Mr. Boland, who had withdrawn to the dining-room off the veranda, and who could now be seen like an immense, pale, benignant spirit of plenty brooding over a well-furnished table, was whispering with a return of his boyish enthusiasm, doubtless to the smart little body:

"Everything ready, Mrs. Smith? Yes-yes; bring out all you've got! Ha, the cookies! Good!"

I'll swear there was a conspiracy between them which had the shocking effect of defrauding the manager's wife of good things cooked in honour of her return!

I caught a glimpse of a neat little woman with an immense white teapot in one hand while the other held a clumped mountain range of golden rock-cakes tipped with black currants. My canvas shoe, now spatless (1 was never seen in them), nudged Dick's canvas bulge. He opened his eyes and grinned happily. 1 read in his expression: "What a dear old chap!" and sent back: "I'll say he is!"

Very soon we were sitting round that table - gorging; there's no other word for it: and when Mr. Boland was at last convinced of our fullness, he expressed great interest in our pathetic adventures.

"And what did you do," he asked; "when you eventually found the car? You lost it once, didn't you?"

"Drank!" said Dick with a currant bun near his mouth.

"Held a council of war -" I began. " -ter!" put in Dick.

Mr. Boland smiled sadly. "Of course," he said, "your water was with the car. Dear me!" and he looked over his spectacles at Dick.

"Don't forget, Richard," I admonished, "what the gentleman said in Townsville - or was it Mackay? - that Charles Lamb said a pun was the lowest form of 'iggerance.' "

"Wasn't it the lowest form of wet?" offered our host with a chuckle.

"Some more buns?" said the housekeeper, who might justly have added, "and no more puns, please!" returning with a filled teapot and glancing cheerfully at the empty plate whereon a few minutes earlier had been the cookies. But the minutes of day were passing; there was no more time to eat, had that been possible; and we rose and returned to the veranda once more eager to be on our way.

Mr. Boland said what amounted to this: "I can't help you, because I don't know this country; and even if we had natives to spare here, I couldn't lend you one without the manager's permission. Therefore, get to Curraghmore cattle-station; there you will find the Roberts family. Curraghmore may not be out of your way; indeed, I think you can find a short cut back to the neighbourhood of the Cooktown Crossing without returning this way. The Curraghmore people will probably give you a guide; be certain they will do their very best for you, for they are very fine people. No, I will not accept payment for the few drops of petrol I've given you; there are only two gallons, and Mrs. Smith can get some more tomorrow from the lorry-driver if she wants to use the iron. And don't thank me again. I have done the very least I can do."

Without the pen of Dickens, who knew precisely how to make alive for his readers all the charm, love, and beauty in gentlemen like Mr. Boland, I can only say in duet with Dick, "Dear old chap!"

There were twenty miles between us and Curraghmore, but these were over a surprisingly excellent, white, slightly sandy bush road; and, pausing for a few minutes at the poor dead old town of Carbine, where we heartened the inn-keeper by drinking a pot of ale with him, we pursued our way across various tributaries of the Mitchell until evening found us just outside the garden gates of Curraghmore homestead.

I am now in a quandary. I am faced with Dick, who adores the Roberts family root and branch, as I do; Dick, who will say, "Ingrate, are you going to rush past the people of Curraghmore who did so much for us?" But more seriously am I faced with the long journey yet before us-and we are not yet at Cooktown! Therefore, I can only attempt an impression.

A beautiful garden-hibiscus and not too much hibiscus, of which one tires in the tropics, amaryllis, zinnias, pink roses, jasmine, and dim mandarin trees laden with golden-red fruit; all the soft perfume of many flowers blending at once with the rich smell of freshly watered earth; garden herbs-mint, thyme, sage, and sweet marjoram; a house on extremely tall piles rising like a gigantic flower in the garden, a house with a gracious tropical veranda. Through the arranged pot-plants and baskets of ferns and coloured shrubs hanging beneath the veranda, we see lights. Evidently the Curraghmore folks spend their days "under the house," ascending to the house proper when the heat of the day has passed. As we approach, the bungalow seems to grow in size; it is now like an immense multi-legged insect wading in a pool of beauty.

The house, we learned later - it was too dark to see that evening - stands near the banks of the McLeod River, now with possibly a foot or two of running water in it - the gentle, placid, innocent looking McLeod, which during the months between December and April may become within a few hours a veritable Campbell for treachery, rising rapidly and turning the whole visible world into a swirling rush of killing water.

To our car have come Bert and Willie Roberts.

All that the former has is ours - at once, for are we not sportsmen and cheerful? All that the latter has *will* be ours, too; but only when he has charmingly fanned us to sleep (he thinks) and X-rayed us to see if we are really well-meaning and straight. We pass; there are no unpleasant "findings," and, a bell ringing, we enter the Curraghmore dining-room and the hearts of the Roberts of Curraghmore.

The great oil lamp on the long dining-table shines on the rosy cheeks and kindly eyes of two daughters and a daughter-in-law. It brightens the carefully brushed hair of the station-hand and a jackeroo; it is on the tow-coloured hair of Dick and his new friend Bert (both nearly of an age, and both of the species which gives its last sixpence to plausible rascals); it brings out the classical features and silver hair of "Willie"; but its most gracious office is performed when it shines on Mrs. Roberts of Curraghmore - Mrs. Roberts of Curraghmore, with her snowy hair, her neat little figure in the well-cut bodice and skirt of black silk relieved by some white lace near the throat; Mrs. Roberts with the quiet gentle voice to whom I, who seldom listen, listen.

But wait! I am not throwing at my hostess, who is past seventy, the patronizing affection of comparative youth for dignified age., She is a wee wisp of a woman, but she herself holds and indeed controls nearly four hundred square miles of cattle country, and without even referring to her well-kept books she can tell in a second the price paid for any item in the station store. She maintains her position not merely by right, but simply because she is clever and able enough to hold it; and her family not only love her, but respect and admire her. Lucky Mrs. Roberts of Curraghmore! I wonder how many of us realize how intensely our elderly parents dislike that "dear old mother," "dear old dad," patronizing affection we fling at them. Who wants to be a back number?

The meal ends; the young ladies help a little with the table-clearing, although there are native servants without; we stroll in the garden, and later return to the living-room, where Dick, with a large piece of white paper, works out a route over the Byerstown with Bert to guide him. Bert drove a dray over the range six or seven years ago, and he went with the driver of the big car which made the unsuccessful attempt to reach Cooktown not very long since; he is obviously a gold-mine to Dick. Our friends agree to lend us one of their native stockmen to guide us at least on to the cattle-pad; they have inspected our store-list and improved it; moreover, the native girls are busy cleaning a kerosene-tin for our water, and even four gallons of petrol are produced. I try to help with the map Dick is making, but gradually I drift to a corner of the long room and find myself listening to a story which began in the very room we are sitting in, and at almost the same time in the evening. Mrs. Roberts sits near, but she says very little; and, curiously, while one hears and sees the terrible picture unfold, one is not conscious of any human sound, certainly not of the soft voices retailing the story. But one hears the patter of rain, the rush of waters, the scream of the wind tearing through space like an express at a million miles an hour. It was in that very room, now so still and peaceful in the balmy tropical night, where Dick is saying to Bert," And we'll find water a hundred yards north of the pad - see, I'll mark it!" that the danger began.

First pools began to form on the cement floor outside the door, but the rain had ceased, and, although suspiciously heavy, the atmosphere was still. Dinner was over, and the family remained in the dining-room, one of its members busy at the sewing-machine on a new summer frock. Then rain began falling again; little waves swept under the door and receded; they returned, and remained! There was an inch of water on the dining-room floor ; the inch became four inches; it grew to a foot; it doubled-there were three feet of water on the dining-room floor; but the family had retreated to the floor above, carrying what little they could in the time. Soon a slight breeze was felt. "This," thought the family, noting that the water had filled the lower. rooms and was actually lapping the floor of their last place of refuge, " will probably kill the rain ; the McLeod will go down."

They had need to hope this, for within hundreds of miles there was no chance of help.

But the breeze became a wind, the wind became a gale, and the gale became a mighty rushing hurricane. It is hard to give an impression of a hurricane. My own sensations during a hurricane which I went through on a Pacific island were of a rushing train bearing down on one at inconceivable speed, threatening to iron one out, and only just falling short of the threat. I was behind cement walls; the women of Curraghmore were on the sheltered side of a wooden veranda!

Half the roof went; a sea got up on the vast lake surrounding the house; great l ogs began crashing against its sturdy piles; at one moment, during a flash of lightning, the women saw the immense tank on tall struts near the homestead bow solemnly and join the rushing procession of yellow water, fallen timber, dead beasts, and wreckage. They clung there, these women, in their soaked garments; they clung there all through one night. There could have been no hope; nothing but death sooner or later faced them. And yet, this thing passed!

The story ended. The soft voices continued.

Dick had reached Cooktown - on paper; but I was searching for some effect on these people of their awful experience, signs of nerviness in the way of twitching fingers or badly controlled eye¬lids. There was nothing, nothing but rosy cheeks, clear eyes, and a perfectly placid outlook on life, with a touch of humour which removed it as far from the bovine as the North Pole is removed from the South.

Dick and I often talked of the Roberts family during the weeks which followed. We sent Mrs. Roberts telegrams from different points on our journey; and when I reached Curraghmore in the story I was writing for the *Sydney Mail* I took up my pen with vast enthusiasm. Indeed, I wrote the above for her. Alas, she never read what I have written about her. One of her daughters wrote to us a few months later explaining that her mother had passed away some weeks after we reached Cape York. Such is the isolation of Curraghmore that, although she was greatly interested in our progress, she did not hear of our success.

The passage of the Stewart River - Note the sweep of the wheel tracks.

7

We attack the Byerstown Range

ALTHOUGH they could hardly spare him, our Curraghmore friends lent us their Douglas to guide us back across country to the Cooktown Crossing and on to the cattle-pad. Douglas, a native stockman, was something of a character In reporting him, I will not inflict his "pidgin."

When our little caravan was packed adequately for the journey next morning, we took up a position in the great station-yard while Douglas chose a horse from the few dozen waiting in a stockyard. Before choosing, he had approached us and said, "You must follow me closely; I will find good places for the car to pass, and you will make pictures of me!"

Nothing, of course, would have given us greater pleasure than to photograph Douglas on his waler guiding us from Curraghmore; but when the great chestnut brute, more than seventeen hands, saw the car, he simply flung up his forefeet in horror and stood on his hind-legs. Douglas then approached backwards, and successfully, too, for a few paces, until the waler smelt us. Then he stood on his head! Douglas tried him all ways, even sideways; but the waler eventually took the matter into his own hands and vaulted the fence, making off down a slope below the homestead. This was our way, and so we followed.

There was now no road, simply a succession of bridle-tracks; but we made the descent very comfortably to a valley in which we found Douglas making circles near a watercourse. He beckoned to us to approach, and we did so; but when we were within twenty yards of the waler, he made one wild rush up the side of a low hill. We were following on low gear until we saw Douglas shaking his head. We paused. At terrific speed the waler then flew down the side of another hill, puffing out steam and foam as a joy-wheel horse would puff if it could. We followed.

"Ogord! "yelled Douglas (a favourite expression), "not here - go back"

And so we returned to the valley. Here we watched Douglas trying to approach in coils. Finally, seeing how hopeless it was for him ever to reach us, I left the car and walked towards him very delicately. It seemed to me that the waler might very well associate me with the smelly, devilish contrivance I had been sitting in.

"Ogord!" said Douglas; "this horse doe s not like the motor-car; I'll go back and get another; you wait!" And off he went.

He returned about an hour later with another horse. I fear we were hardly more popular with the new waler; but she - it was a mare now, merely showed her distaste by trotting stiffly like a carriage horse, with her mouth wide open and her nostrils distended, and evidently determined to pull the arms of Douglas out by the roots.

"Ogord! " said Douglas; "she is better; you will make pictures soon."

Followed two or three hours of rather weary driving across dried-up country to the Disali River, a tributary of the Mitchell. Still, we were making progress, and that cheered us.

I think I have mentioned before that a large car made an attempt some time before our appearance to open up motor communication between Mt. Molloy and Cooktown via Curraghmore. Bert Roberts had told us that the driver of this car had a very bad time at the Disali, trying to get up the annoying sand-hill which forms the far bank. He used up much of his petrol (which he could not afford) and spent a day and a night fighting the Disali. He finally submitted to being dragged up by horses.

We could neither afford time nor petrol. But here our New Zealand experience helped us. Innocent of what is called "bush experience" in Australia, we are both experts with sand. We have lived in the vicinity of the Ninety Mile Beach; indeed, I lived on the actual beach for nearly nine months, and during that time I often helped cars out of mortal difficulty. I wonder if I shall be useful or merely boring if I offer here what I know about motoring over sand, especially where quicksand is likely to occur. Without our knowledge of sand we could never have reached the end of our journey. The advice I offer will seem obvious; but it outlines a process towards safety which is seldom followed by those who have not learned from bitter experience. I will tabulate.

(a) Never attempt to cross a bad sandy flat without deflating tyres to half their normal pressure; therefore always carry a tyre pressure gauge. A good motorist will dislike deflating his tyres, but so long as they are pumped up to their correct pressure when the sand has been passed, no harm is done either to the tubes or covers. On the other hand much harm may be done to an engine forced to struggle without tyre deflation.

(b) If the sand is soft, and rises in a serious slope, count ten! Then carefully make a good track up the slope with tree branches, strips of bark and grass. Give the track exquisite attention; careless work will defeat itself, for one weak spot will allow the car to lose way, to stop, and, of course, to dig a hole. Do not decide to make the first attempt successful. Run up a little way and back-back quickly. Thus weakness is detected and useful tracks made. If the engine gives out on the slope, never dream of trying to go on; you cannot! Get back, repair any weakness and make another attempt. Never, if possible, reach the struggling stage.

(c) Crossing a sandy flat with patches of quick-sand demands a separate section. We have several times been stuck in quicksand; we have always escaped; and yet quicksand has often spelt the end of fine cars, unnecessarily, I think. A car will not usually sink below the running-boards in quicksand-certainly not in the quicksand likely to be found even where the most dare-devil motorist is travelling. As is well known, quick-sand is usually a layer of ordinary dry-looking sand superimposed on a stratum of what amounts to thick sandy water. When it is walked on, every footprint becomes a tiny pool; when it is jumped on with unpleasant sinkings at each jump, the water seems to gather on the surface. After a time the area ceases to be quicksand, but anything left in the drained sand is gripped as if in a vice. Now the only thing to do with a car is to get each wheel on a clear hard surface. Sacks, grass, straw, branches, or even overcoats under the wheels are quite useless. Each wheel must be jacked up and placed on a board or whatever else can be found. Something can always be found. If one wheel is left in even two inches of wet sand, the car will not budge, not matter how furiously the engine tries to make it. Each wheel must be on a hard firm surface with enough room for a start of at least a yard. Of course the jacking up is not easy, but it can usually be done. The process, too, appears a waste of time. Still it is better to waste a few hours making preparations than to footle about with sacks and overcoats under wheels and then to see the car topple over. Which it can do very easily in quicksand.

I must apologize for the above. I know how obvious it all sounds; yet even the most efficient motorists fall badly when confronted with sand.

The Disali looked far from attractive; but, following our rule, we left the car on the near bank and began the work of building a road. The beds of these peninsula rivers are intensely hot. The great boulders can hardly be touched; and the sand is almost on fire. The near bank of the Disali is steep, but it is always possible to get down a river-bank, and so we merely cleared a rough way. We removed a few stones from the bed, fortunately not very sandy, and then began on the sand-bank on the far side, which rose about thirty to forty feet. For nearly two hours we cut and collected branches in terrific heat, and at the end of that time a creditable track had been finished. Unfortunately the grade was very steep and it was therefore necessary to unpack the car; but our care was happily rewarded when the baby ran smartly up the bank and reached the top without very much effort. Our first hurdle had been cleared.

Douglas now led us through the forest without even a bridle-track to guide him; but he soon became expert in finding suitable crossings for the car, and we made excellent progress. The forest was again well populated with kangaroos, walla¬bies, and even emus. The kangaroos were intensely interested in us, more interested than frightened, it seemed. Once I saw an immense kangaroo standing with two of his wives (Douglas said). The ladies apparently wanted to fly, but the gentleman stood his ground bravely, quivering with interest. The little family followed us at a safe distance for a time.

Eventually we reached the Mitchell, and here we filled up our kerosene tin with water, and had a good drink ourselves. I cannot begin to explain how delicious water was becoming. We carried, of course, a canvas water-bag, but the water never seemed to get time to cool. We used to put a grain or two of permanganate of potash in the bag every time we filled it.

We saw our old car tracks, submitting cheerfully to the teasing of Douglas, who soon led us to the cattle-pad. The cattle-pad proved to be a series of four or five wide bridle-tracks running more or less parallel, but spreading or narrowing when trees, rocks, ant-heaps, or other obstacles made that necessary.

We crossed Rice Creek, an unpleasant gully of big stones, and the scene of disaster to Bert Roberts when he was driving a dray across it some years ago. His dray "capset" Douglas said. On we went, rushing furiously along at about four miles an hour and sometimes even five-on high gear. It takes a good driver to drive a car at this speed on "high," and motorists will appreciate the great saving in petrol, so vitally necessary to us. The end of that day saw us on the near bank of a great dry creek called Spring Creek, and, following our invariable rule never to attempt sleep with a difficulty left unsurmounted, we prepared to cross it. But Douglas, who had said once or twice during the late afternoon, "Don't you blokes ever spell?" explained that he knew a much simpler crossing farther north, which could be very well kept for the morning, since it would require no work. He had imagined that crossing; but as I said before, Douglas was a character. He added considerably to our joy that night, when he said to me with rather a puzzled expression in his dark eyes, "Say - don't you blokes ever swear " Which gave a startling impression of the other friends of Douglas!

Camping, now that we had no tent, was a simple business. Dick arranged the beds - gum-leaves in goodly or not goodly quantities, much depending upon whether the day had been fatiguing or not, with the rugs on top. We invariably undressed and slept in pyjamas; it made for freshness in the morning. The evenings were warm enough now; but before dawn it' often became cold. We always tried to get the great mosquito-net arranged and tucked under the blankets before sunset; snakes have a habit of crawling under rugs. We had heard several stories of bushmen rolling up small snakes in their swags.

While Dick attended to the bedroom and car department, I cooked the dinner. Mrs. Roberts had given us two loaves of bread and a joint of cooked salt beef. This first evening we had salt beef and potatoes and bread-and-butter with tea. We carried some packets of dried apples, and these we chewed uncooked. I liked the salt beef very well, but it gave me heart-burn. Frankly, indigestion is a complaint I know nothing of, and for some weeks I had regarded the pain near my chest as rheumatism, also unknown to me. A good woman on a station farther north quickly diagnosed my complaint and miraculously cured it with something she took from a small tin. I think it was baking-powder.

Of course Douglas interested us very much.

We are used to Maoris, and we found amusement in comparing the two races. Douglas was born with, and has apparently lived all his life near, whites. Dick liked him better than I did, and without doubt he was very use-

useful to us. My feelings towards him were closely akin to those of that New England widower returned from the funeral of his wife. "Yes," said he, in reply to the sympathetic remarks offered by friends; "she was a good wife, a splendid mother and a pillar of the church - *but I didn't like her!*" Douglas was an efficient guide who saved us much digging by his almost uncanny discovery of good crossings over the many little watercourses and ditches which always run about even the best bush; moreover, although lightly built, he was strong, and his weight helped us up the banks of creeks where, without it, we might have worked for hours: that he was useful is undeniable, as it is equally true that I, at any rate, found his presence something of a restraint. I was relieved when he left us, possibly because of the unusual humility which his bush knowledge introduced, or more probably because I believed Dick and I would have much more fun and excitement fighting the Byerstown alone!

To quote Douglas as a typical Australian native would be absurd. It has been my good fortune to know intimately most of the native races in the South Seas; and to say that the Australian aboriginal is of the lowest race of mankind is to confess palpable ignorance of him and a slavish devotion to an old-fashioned obsession. For in the rough he is a fine fellow - clever, devoted, courageous, and with a most vivid sense of humour far far above the sense of fun most natives naturally possess. But Douglas, although a full-bred black, seemed in no sense an aboriginal; he was more, I thought, a dark mirror reflecting the images of some dozen white drovers in moods varying from sombre desperation to wild hilarity - a sedulous ape, still a useful kind of ape, aping to perfection his gods, the white drovers. The cattle-pad, driving mobs of cattle, the bush, the finding of water and its condition when found - black, green, cloudy or clear; making damper or johnny-cakes, freezing at night and scorching by day; stampedes - all the life of the cattle man in Queensland was the life of Douglas, and I think he consciously liked it. But to me his naivete narrowly escaped insolence, and his inquisitive friendliness, in which there was no particle of respect, often ran very close to impertinence. He had said the water in Spring Creek was good, and I had replied, "Then we shan't have to boil it or put Condy's in it." "D'you think," said he furiously, "I'd tell you the water was good when it's bad? I don't want to poison you!" And he turned sulkily on his heel. That, of course, was not meant to be offensive. Douglas was aping a dyspeptic drover after a bad night.

Occasionally, however, the lovable native emerged. "D'you know what I'm going to do with that ten bob you left at Curraghmore for me?" he asked. We were duly inquisitive. "Well" said he; "I'm going to buy my girl a cake of scented soap and a red handkerchief." Just before we bade him good-bye he remarked dreamily, "I've been trying to guess what you blokes are going to send me as a present from Sydney: I'm pretty certain it will be a watch!" "Ogord!" was his favourite exclamation, reaching us at odd momnts and expressed without fury, rather in the melancholy tones of a washer-woman *in extremis*.

We were up before dawn the next morning on the banks of Spring Creek. I prepared breakfast while Dick packed the car; Douglas was concerned in catching his horse. By the time the tall gums around us were silhouetted against the glow of a rosy dawn, all seemed ready for the day's adventure. Despite our inexperience and a moderately humble knowledge of it, despite the fact that we carried no effective spares and that everything depended upon the little car's ability to bear the strain of the roughest cross-country work, we were in excellent spirits, for now Cooktown stood at the end of a track we might follow. The Curraghmore folks had said we *might* get through, and even Douglas had allowed that, if we did not get lost, if the car did not collapse, and if we did not break our necks or get bitten by snakes, we should reach Cooktown.

Personally I had no doubt, until I heard Dick say, "We're buggered, now!"

I went over to him.

"Someone," he went on, "has stood on our back tyre!" and he pointed to the flattened cover. "We can mend it, surely?" I questioned, rather puzzled at Dick's concern.

"We could," he admitted, "if *all* the solution had not leaked out of the tube," and he showed me the flattened tube that he had taken from the tyre-repair outfit tin.

The tube had evidently been slightly defective, but not dangerously so until great heat had made the solution almost like water. It seemed quite empty. To make matters much worse, the spare tyre had been punctured some days earlier and had not been mended. Almost automatically I had jacked up the rear axle and had taken off the wheel.

"We've got one chance," said Dick, pointing to what was hardly more than a black gluey stain near the bottom of the solution tube, which he had split open; "if that will dissolve in petrol, it might hold."

Fortunately the black stain made the petrol cloudy; we applied it, and, thank God, it held. Moreover, although in similar and even better country north of Cooktown, when we had adequate repair stores, we sometimes averaged ten punctures a day, yet until we reached Cooktown after crossing the Byerstown, which was literally alive with twigs hard as iron and grass-straw dried hard like steel, we had no more punctures.

Had we been engaged on a reliability test, had we been employed by car agents or manufacturers to advertise, it might not have mattered so much; but that prospective buyer on Thursday Island would never give a good price for a car which had been running on rough country with tyres stuffed with grass or sand. We tried never to lose sight of the future in present troubles!

We crossed Spring Creek without much difficulty and pursued our way along the pad, climbing low hills, passing along their tops, and descending to the inevitable small dry creek or watercourse which occassionally demanded much work whenever Douglas failed to find a good crossing. Sometimes the land was bare and infertile; the eucalyptus-tree was never absent and we were always in the bush; but occasionally the cattle-pads were fringed with dry grass four feet high;; it can therefore be imagined what our position would have been in the event of a bush-fire. During this day we saw no game.

Although the crossing of the Byerstown Range presented what occasionally seemed insuperable difficulties; although it demanded the most magnificent driving and car-mastership, offered by my friend in full measure (1 never drove after we left the roads); although it was considered in the North a great piece of work, and nearly flattened us out mentally and physically; 1 feel that the story of our daily struggle will bore my readers more than it can interest them. 1 must therefore hurry on with the knowledge that 1 may not, as 1 cannot, describe one-tenth of our struggles. Not that struggles worried either of us much; our laughter could be heard well above the beat of that glorious little British engine.

At noon, after travelling for upwards of four hours, we reached the Kelly St. George River. We had accomplished six miles! Here Douglas left us, taking a short cut back to Curraghmore over a mountain. He had offered to help us across the Kelly, but, knowing that he was needed at Curraghmore, we thought it best to send him home.

We believed we could now manage.

The St. George River, another tributary of the great Mitchell, winds annoyingly along the cattle-pad, and it must be crossed at least three times. Its tributaries, too, are always cropping up. Locally the St. George is prefixed with Kelly because one Kelly tried cattle-ranching here, building his shack and stockyard near the river-banks where the pad crosses. Apparently the river runs only during the "wet," between December and possibly May; for the rest of the year it offers occasional deep pools almost alive with small fish. Otherwise, it is a gully forty yards wide and thirty or forty feet deep, with a bed of sand and great boulders. The heat in the river-bed was again very great, and the attraction which the pools offer to horses, cattle, and wild animals results in the presence of innumerable small flies, apparently of the house variety. They are quick and persistent, and most eager to get at the water in the eyes. I noticed that the natives give up trying to combat them, often permitting dozens of the pests to concentrate in the corners of their eyes without worrying to swish them away.

It felt a trifle lonely after Douglas had gone, but the Kelly St. George had to be crossed - and we crossed it. This process consisted of a rapid run over a sand-mound at the near bank, an almost perpendicular drop down the side of the sand-mound, a quick run over the stony river-bed, and then two hours' solid work digging and pushing our way up the far bank. We did not mind the work very much; but the flies seized this chance to drink our eyes while our hands were engaged.

After the Kelly, we found traces of the old road. The pad occasionally followed it, but while it was useful sometimes, more often than not it led us into trouble, especially at creek and gully crossings, where its old wheel-ruts had apparently attracted water during forty years and had sometimes become small narrow chasms six and eight feet deep. Fallen timber was often annoying, but ant-heaps, especially where grass grew well, were dangerous.

We were steadily but not very perceptibly climbing to the summit of the Byerstown Range forty miles ahead. Towards the late afternoon the trail improved; and we had actually managed to cover twelve miles during that day when a thunderstorm, the only one we suffered on the entire trip, put an end to the day's work, and we camped.

After an excellent dinner of scones fried in boiling fat, and stewed apples with condensed milk, we were peacefully smoking, feeling very thankful that the thunderstorm had not produced enough rain to fill the creeks and rivers. It was all very comfortable; the twelve miles added to the distance register, and the remarkably small amount of petrol used in covering them made me quite happy, until I observed Dick's first finger chivying a large scorpion which had left one of the rotten logs on the fire.

"Curious bird, that," he was saying, "got pincers like a crab. Hey, don't kill it!" "I always kill scorpions," I said, jamming my feet on four others fortunately too dazed by smoke and heat to be actively dangerous. The place seemed alive with scorpions, and so we called this camp Scorpion Flat.

A short journey the following morning, stumbling over logs and knocking down the ant-heaps we could not avoid, brought us to the banks of the Great St. George - we lived in an atmosphere of St. Georges and disliked it intensely - and to cross this river seemed out of the question. The years with their floods having made the old road ford nothing but a great rocky gulch, we were at a loss to find a way of even getting down to the river-bed. The banks were cliffs of precipitous rock, and apparently could not be descended without days of labour. Fortunately we were able to work a little way along a spur up the river, and this took us to within fifteen feet of the sandy bed below. A chance had to be taken here. Attaching block and tackle to the rear axle of the car, and using a convenient tree, Dick was able to drive safely to the bottom. In view of what happened a few hours later it is amazing that the rope holding the tackle to the rear axle held, for the strain must have been very great. Had this rope broken then, nothing could have saved the car from crashing to the bottom and turning turtle. I should imagine Dick would have been killed. We ran cheerfully along the river-bed, and, the far bank being an easy grade - there are always compensations! - we were soon on our way, making for the next St. George - actually the same river achieving an annoying elbow-like bend. It was not possible to go round. Here we very nearly reached the end of our journey. I am about to relate another proof of our car's humanity, or super-humanity.

We had descended to the river-bed without trouble; we had even managed to climb up on to the first ledge of the far bank. Then for the final climb it was necessary to run back along this ledge a few yards. I will try to make the picture clear. The little car was actually facing a very steep rise of about forty feet. A few yards behind her the bank dropped sheer to the river-bed ten feet below. The bank at this point was actually concave, where the water had swept round a bend in the river, which was now quite dry. Block and tackle were necessary because the grade was steep, and the surface was sand and sandstone rubble, into which the back wheels dug without making progress. While I worked the tackle, Dick drove; and we managed to get half-way up. But here the car stopped, the back wheels spinning madly, almost burning the sand. Some other way had to be found.

We chocked the car carefully, knowing that, if once she began backing, nothing could save her from destruction if she fell over the steep ledge at the bottom of the slope.

We now attempted a most dangerous scheme.

Dick left the car, and we tried to haul her up inch by inch with the tackle. I was on top of the rise, hauling near the tree which held the tackle; Dick was a few feet lower down than the car.

She began to move slowly; a few more feet, and the worst would be over. The rope was singing with the strain. Steadily we pulled; and then I heard a mighty crack. The rope had broken!

I rushed to the car. I saw Dick get behind her to hold her. I saw him knocked flat. Even I saw him roll miraculously out of the way; and, it is true, I thanked God in those seconds. The little car was gathering speed, but I reached her. I gripped the front mudguards and rushed with her, exerting all my strength with the idea of keeping her straight. Nothing, I believed, could save her; but I knew it would be less bad for her to make that final and awful jump back-on rather than at an angle. We were now going at a great pace. The back wheels reached the ledge; I let go, and over the bank flew the little car. It was all a matter of seconds; Dick was running down to me when. the last leap was made.

I wonder if anyone will believe me; but it is perfectly true that the car avoided all the rocks in that river-bed and landed fairly and squarely on her wheels, on one of the few sand-mounds which rose up from among the rocks. Except for a cracked spring leaf, which we soon tied with wire, she was undamaged.

I have, I know, laboured in telling of this incident. But I am conscious of emotion as I write. Had Dick been seriously hurt, I could not have left him to the mercy of ants and dingoes while I sought help; there was no chance in the world of anyone seeking us within many weeks; and we were now thirty miles from Curraghmore. Had the car been smashed, it would have meant an end to our project, and temporary financial ruin.

It was not the rope of our block and tackle which parted. It was some very pretty silver-coloured rope we had bought farther south and which bound the pulley to the axle. I shall always distrust pretty rope, and I will never be concerned in drawing a car up a hill without towing a stout log behind as a chock.

After this excitement we walked more warily; we simply set to work to improve the track, and after a time we made the grade.

There were many tributaries of the St. George to cross, and creeks and watercourses appeared about every two or three hundred yards; but the end of that day saw us happily encamped at a place called Knobbys. To stockmen, Knobbys is a glorious oasis in the Byerstown Range desert. Actually water is not seriously scarce on this trail; but except at Knobbys it is never clear or very clean. The creek at Knobbys is rather like an English brook, running between green banks or dropping over rocks and boulders. I cannot begin to explain what it meant to us. First we drank to our hearts' content, and without the reserve which had been so necessary since we had left Curraghmore. We let all the water run out of the radiator and filled it up. We felt the little car deserved a good drink. Then we had our evening meal of boiled eggs, stewed apples, and bread-and-butter. Most of the evening was spent in the creek bogeying our own filthy dust-specked bodies, washing towels, and all spare clothing, and finally cleansing all cooking and eating utensils. On the journey water could never be spared for the dishes.

This creek runs across what is a great swamp during th"wet." We saw many deep pools and lagoons. They were often alight with waterlilies and lotus blossoms.

Unfortunately the pad again becomes indefinite on the far side of the great swamp, and we had some trouble in finding it again. Indeed I must confess that we spent five good hours following a wrong trail, which happily ended at a precipice down which we could not drop. We were seriously bushed for a time; but by returning to the swamp and carefully reconnoitering by compass, we eventually found the pad running with the old road, which was quite respectable for a few chains.

We had lost much time, but we were determined to reach the Palmer River that night. The Palmer was considered our biggest hurdle. "Once across the Palmer, and you're set!" Bert Roberts had said. The pad and the old road continued pleasantly respectable, and we therefore ignored the setting sun and hunger, pushing on while the going was good. Had a wandering stockman met us, he would have been vastly astonished. The little car picking her way slowly through the bush, with her brilliant headlights shining a long way ahead, must have created a curious picture. I walked ahead, knocking down ant-heaps and clearing fallen timber from the pad.

At about nine o'clock the old road attempted to go round a hill, but fell away so badly that we thought it best to camp. We were on the near side of the great Palmer River valley. We had accomplished six miles that day.

It was a great night. We were very tired indeed; my heartburn, not shared by Dick, who had refused the salt beef, was annoying; but I found no difficulty in cooking a pair of big fat curlew shot that afternoon. Our method of cooking was simple enough. Having cleaned and plucked them efficiently, we broke the birds into small pieces and dusted them with pepper and salt. Then, when the lard in a biscuit tin was boiling furiously we dropped the pieces into it and waited for them to brown. We ate one bird each and invented a new verb. Not a word was spoken; we simply ate. "To palmer" is a verb in our jargon which means to make noises when we eat, or to remain silent at a meal.

The next morning we dropped down a very steep hill to the great river. The crossing of it was not very difficult, and when the car was safely on the far side, we returned to bathe and to drink. During the "wet," the Palmer is a mighty torrent; but when we crossed it we found only a wide valley of sand and rocks with many beautiful pools here and there.

Forty or fifty years ago the neighbourhood of this river could boast a population of nearly twelve thousand; more than fifty tons of gold were taken from the Palmer. There had been many hotels, even along the way we had passed; but from the time we bade farewell to Douglas at the Kelly St. George until we reached Butcher's Hill, we saw no one. There was no one to see.

On then, with the back of our journey broken!

We passed through Old Maitland, which isn't any Maitland at all now; we crossed creek after creek, gully after gully, ditch after ditch, the flies continued to madden us, and the heat was often unbearable; but the end of that blessed day saw us eating a roast turkey (wild) on the top of the Byerstown Range.

The old road, which we had followed occasionally, now became perfectly clear. It had been beautifully cut on the mountain range from sandstone, and even time could not utterly destroy it. Nevertheless it was a terrifying jumble of slabs, which forbade progress, and caused much anxiety and some labour the next morning when we began the descent.

The actual descent of the range is a sharp drop of a few miles; but it would have caused us less trouble had our brakes been in good condition. Constant and abnormal use had caused wearing, and often the car was in danger as she dropped from step to step. One of us was always ready with a chock; often a rope became necessary. However, the descent, which we had feared greatly, occupied only three hours, and we had luncheon under a tree on the banks of the Laura River.

We had mastered the Byerstown Range Road.

Ours was the first car to pass over it, and we were very proud of her. In thinking over what I have written so far, I recall that night in Auckland when Dick and I discussed our trip. Anyone patient enough to have followed me thus far will admit that we were having adventures!

We had still a dozen miles of rough country to cover before reaching Butcher's Hill, but, while there were one or two creeks to cross and some work, the country was very flat. Towards three in the afternoon we were honking our horn near the gates of a stockyard, watching a stout gentleman on a homestead veranda with a pair of binoculars at his eyes, staring vainly in the opposite direction to ours.

To him, it was inconceivable that a car should come over the Byerstown. He was staring towards Cooktown. Finally we saw another man emerge from the homestead. He dashed towards the stout gentleman and pulled his body round towards us. They both came swiftly to our car.

The Earl homestead at Butcher Hill.

8

"Tarred Roads"

THE big man we had seen staring towards Cooktown was Mr. Earl, the owner of Butcher's Hill cattle-station; the other man, who ran from the back regions, was Mr. Jones. Mr. Jones owns a cattle-run of his own; but Mr. Earl's manager had left a trifle suddenly and Mr. Jones was looking after the place until Mr. Earl could find someone else. Mr. Earl - I must apologize for all these proper nouns - lives in Cairns, where, I gathered, he is a very prosperous business man. Both men were considerably astonished to see us, although I thought Mr. Earl showed lack of faith, in that he had persistently stared towards Cooktown when he heard the horn honking. He had been dreaming about a car coming over the Byerstown, he said. But of course, he was not to know that ours is "of the stuff that dreams are made of." I know he will forgive me if, on behalf of comedy, I outline our first engagement, and our only one of a hostile nature. I have not Dick's sang-froid; if anyone annoys me, I let him know at once, especially if it is not feasible for him to hit me. Tired, and suffering reaction after the journey over the Byerstown, I could be annoyed very easily indeed. My sense of humour, if I have one, must have been in abeyance.

 Mr. Earl's first greeting when he reached us was: "Gad! Where have you sprung from?"

 "Over the Byerstown!" we said carelessly.

 Mr. Earl thereupon stared seriously into the eyes of Mr. Jones. "What did I say to you before we turned in?" he asked.

 Mr. Jones shook his head and smiled mysteriously. Mr. Jones is a trifle like the old lady's parrot; he doesn't say much, but he thinks a lot!

 "Oh," said Mr. Earl (we did not know his name then), "my name's Earl; and this is Mr. Jones, my temporary manager." We thereupon shook hands and told him our names.

 "Why, of course," continued Mr. Earl, "I heard of you when you were in Cairns a fortnight ago. Oh yes - quite!" He looked at us with approval (I hope) and went on; and at this point a sense of humour left me -

"You see," said Mr. Earl, " here have been so many wild adventurers dashing about Australia - stunt artists, jugglers, and the like, that people are getting rather shy, and you would not meet -"

"What a loss," I said coldly -" for the shy people!"

I had to do it; I had to stamp on someone. Dick and I had exchanged a few mild shots coming down the Byerstown and a few more just before lunch at the Laura River; but they had not exhausted my magazine of bile. And in any case I felt sorry for the adventurers, stunt artists, jugglers, and the like nipping round Australia. Dick and I could not afford to put up at a smart Cairns hotel. But if we had stayed at the leading inn and cut a dash, doubtless we could have borrowed as much money as we liked; we should, too, have met the Cairns elite. As a matter of fact Cairns had been very, very kind to us; I doubt if the town could have offered us anyone more charming and delightful than the M.O., the matron, the newspaper editor, Mr. Thorn, and Constable Pitchem.

But I do not think the good Mr. Earl had noticed me. He was concerned with us as a startling, and I think pleasant, incident rather than as persons.

"What did I tell you, Mr. Jones," he repeated, "before we turned in?"

Again Mr. Jones shook his mysterious head.

"I said to him," continued Mr. Earl - " I said to him -' Mr. Jones, what would you have thought if I'd turned up in a car - from Cairns - over the Byerstown? '

"We spent quite a long time this morning," went on Mr. Earl, "discussing the possibility of getting a car through. It was my last thought before sleeping; and here I am awakened by a car which has got through."

At this moment I gained the preposterous notion that by some magical process Mr. Earl was trying to fit his body into our car during the trip; I could not see how she could possibly hold him, and felt anxious about the springs.

"And that little car did it? Well, well! " he continued. "She got over the Byerstown first; and look at her, Mr. Jones -"

Mr. Jones looked and nodded, showing great approval by moving his pipe from one side of his mouth to the other.

"She might," said Mr. Earl, " have come out of a showcase!"

I was immediately pleased. If Mr. Earl could think that, then the purchaser on Thursday Island might also be impressed. Mr. Earl, I saw at once, was an excellent fellow (which he is). It was stupid of me to have been curt about the jugglers; doubtless a juggler had been pinching his sugar-cane or something! But the sense of humour again flew when, in what I thought patronizing tones, he said thoughtfully:

"Yes, a wonderful little car! I've often seen them nipping about Sydney - *great town cars!*"

My hand stole towards my sword at that - " great *town* cars!"

Stroking his chin thoughtfully, and smiling (my jaundiced mind decided) like the tiger with the lady inside it, he walked round the car and remarked: "Yes, I've often said that if ever I live in a town with good cement or tarred roads in its neighbourhood, I'll get one of these little cars; with good cement roads - or even tarred - you can't beat 'em!"

Out came my sword!

"Tarred roads and cement be damned, sir! " said I. "Hasn't this car just proved to you that she can go over the roughest country in the world and be in good condition at the end? Hasn't she been where no other car has been? Didn't a great foreign car try it more than a year ago - and how far did she get? Twelve miles - to the Kelly St. George! Faugh!"

"That car didn't even get to the Kelly," said Dick quietly; "she reached the near side of Spring Creek."

"Oh yes, yes - quite - of course - a wonderful little car - and British!" continued Mr. Earl, in no way affected by my irritation. "I have," he went on kindly, "a -- and a --," and he mentioned two rich American brands of car; "but as I say, if ever I live in a city with tarred roads - "

"Come and have a cup of tea! " urged Mr. Jones quickly (one of his few remarks), thus saving good Mr. Earl from instant death; for I'll swear I would have loosened the car brakes and let her run over him - to see if he were tarred or cemented.

Dick seemed to think I had been unnecessarily rude, pointing out that, if it was natural for Mr. Earl to believe that small cars were only fit for tarred roads, he would believe that because it was Nature, and, of course, you couldn't go against Nature!

Butcher's Hill is an immense cattle-run, some hundreds of square miles. Much of the land is magnificent-rich black soil-and near the homestead are several springs offering enough sweet water to irrigate home pastures. The result is a fine vegetable garden. But I cannot admit being impressed with cattle-ranching in Queensland in these days. Of course the great drawback in most of Queensland is the lack of rain. When we were at Butcher's Hill they had not had a drop of rain for more than seven months. The grass was sometimes four feet high, but burnt hard and dry. During the wet, the cattle cannot possibly eat a millionth part of the food offered, but soon after the dry begins the grass gets baked hard, and the cattle keep near the few springs and water-holes. Mr. Earl had been mustering his thoroughbred Hereford bulls, and they, poor fellows, were half dead, hardly able to walk. He said that a week or two after the rain began, all the cattle not dead of hunger and thirst would pick up magnificently. I think it was Mr. Earl who told us that beasts, even old beasts, who had been worn almost to skeletons during the dry, offered tender beef, like veal, when fattened up a few weeks after the wet season began. I do not know whether to believe him or not! I incline to the "not."

The land seems to' be held on a lease system, although a square mile can be, or used to be, free-hold. Land is not bought in the ordinary way. The cattle are bought, and the land, plant, and homestead are thrown in. Buyers sometimes drive the cattle to where they want them, and immediately forget the land, the plant, and the homestead. It would not be hard to forget the homesteads! While romantic-looking in some ways, those we saw were not palatial. Cattle-ranching is a poor sort of business these days, and the money made from cattle can hardly make up for the sad isolation in which cattlemen live. And the poor fellows do not seem to be making more than labourers' wages. I do not know this subject well enough to say anything very much about it; but on the whole I should prefer a small chicken farm of three acres to a cattle-station of three hundred square miles. The hens at Butcher's Hill, incidentally, were doing remarkably well. The late manager's housekeeper had looked after them, breeding white leghorns, and the result was two or three dozen eggs entering the homestead storeroom every day. Most of them were wasted.

Mr. Jones, who, like many Queensland cattlemen, is an excellent cook and very clean housekeeper, boiled twenty eggs for the four of us. When

Mr. Earl saw them on the table he said, " D'you think you've boiled enough eggs?" Mr. Earl was jesting; but Mr. Jones saw no joke, and boiled sixteen more. I ate six; Dick managed eight! In addition, we were offered cold salt beef and great rich sweet potatoes. It was a fine spread. But even more delightful were the two comfortable beds we were given that night. Sleeping out on the ground is all right in many ways, but it does not prevent a man enjoying a conventional bed occasionally.

Cooktown was fifty miles to the east of us ; it was not on our direct route to Cape York, but on behalf of glory we thought we might as well claim the honour of being the first car to enter the city. There was a rumour flying about the bush that the driver of the first car would be given a bonus of £50 by the fathers of the city, and it seemed to us that if £50 were a-begging we might as well have it. Actually our direct route lay north, to a settlement called Laura. I insist on this point because we have to make excuses a little later on!

Mr. Earl was riding in to Cooktown the next morning, and we regretted being unable to offer him a lift. The car was already dangerously overladen, and Mr. Earl is a big man. As I said to him, "We could do it, Mr. Earl, if only you had tarred roads or cement boulevards in your neighbourhood!"

However, we waited for him at Springvale, where we lunched with Mr. Roberts, an uncle of our Curraghmore friends, and he caught up to us at King's Plains, where we all spent the night with the Gibsons. The next morning, Dick discharged me a couple of miles out of Cooktown and motored quickly back to pick up Mr. Earl. We stowed him across the baggage on the back seat, with his feet emerging at one side and his head sticking out at the other, and together we drove triumphantly into Cooktown.

When we drove into Cooktown it seemed asleep, but when we drew up at the Commercial Hotel, a few heads looked out from doors and windows; the inevitable small boys gathered round, and Mrs. Wallace, who owns the hotel, rushed out in some anxiety. She could see only the head and shoulders of Mr. Earl emerging from under the cotton awning of the little car, and she thought maybe an accident had reduced him to just that much. We had some ado to get Mr. Earl out, but, when we did, he put us right with the population, including Mrs. Wallace, who is his sister. Mr Earl introduced us to the elders of the city, and never failed to tell each of them that (a) we were genuine, and that (b) a few hours before our arrival he had dreamt us. I could not see how we could be false; and I had again that preposterous notion that the Baby would have to carry Mr. Earl retrospectively over the Byerstown. And I knew he weighed about sixteen stone !

Once more economy had to be thought of. The car required overhauling and the brakes relining; it would mean about five days in Cooktown. Therefore a camping-place had to be found. It is possible to buy a bungalow for about £25 in Cooktown; hotels are slightly dearer; but we thought we would not buy an hotel that day, and so we asked if we might rent a small cottage.

Good Charles Petching, the Town Clerk and known throughout the North as the King of Cooktown, placed us in some rooms behind his office, and we were soon very comfortable.

We inquired discreetly about the £50 bonus.

It was really a matter of no importance, we explained. The money meant nothing; the honour - everything! But there were no fifty pounds forthcoming. Cooktown is about dead, although I think the little town will revive when times are better. Neither the Town Council nor the County Council had promised any £50; as far as I could make out, Mr. Earl had promised to give that sum to the motor mailman for road improvement if he pushed through. The whole incident was a little sad to us!

Of course our arrival created some excitement in the town. Although we wanted to push on within a few days, fearing thunder showers in the Peninsula, we agreed to stay a little longer when the elders explained that Senator Foll and Doctor Nott, two prominent politicians, were arriving to make them vote the right way. The idea of the Cooktowners was to produce us as direct evidence that the Byerstown Range Road was possible for motor traffic with some money spent in repairs, to help to point out that their really very sad way to extinction as Cooktowners could only be blocked effectively by the removal of the strangle-hold killing them - no road communication with the rest of Australia.

Senator Foll and Doctor Nott duly arrived, and a meeting of the Cooktown Progress Association was called. Without many clothes, we had some difficulty in making ourselves presentable; I know I could only face people with any degree of certainty:-

> When you wear a cloudy collar and a shirt that isn't white,
> And you cannot sleep for thinking how you'll reach tomorrow night,
> You may be a man of sorrow, and on speaking terms with Care,
> But as yet you're unacquainted with the Demon of Despair;
> For I rather think that nothing heaps the trouble on your mind
> Like the knowledge that your trousers badly need a patch behind.

However, Mrs. Wallace of the Commercial Hotel helped us out here, and, when the time came, we were more or less ready. I liked the names, Senator Foll and Doctor Nott. What curious chance brought them together? The only trouble I found was to say their names correctly when my turn came to speak. It was difficult to remember which name was attached to senator and which to doctor.

"And now, gentlemen, I have much pleasure in introducing the two New Zealanders who have driven the first car to Cooktown!" The chairman of the Cooktown Progress Association glanced towards Dick and me near his right. "They," he added a little nervously, "will both address you."

"What about it, old man?" I whispered.

Dick hunched his shoulders, struggled back into his chair, blushed or flushed violently, and, fixing me with a cold eye, muttered, " I *won't!*" And I knew he wouldn't.

I therefore rose and made a most killing speech, calculated, it must have seemed, to destroy everyone present. And yet my object was most worthy. It was simply to fascinate Senator Foll and Doctor Nott, and through them to drag money from the Treasury for Cooktown's sorry need, and also to inspire the Progress Association to even greater efforts.

"Mr. Chairman-Senator Noll, Doctor Fott: gentlemen- "

"Not-Noll! *Foll,* you owl! " whispered Dick with a nudge; "and not Fott - *Nott!*" "I beg your pardon, Dick," I said seriously and aloud, looking at him reproachfully; "did you say anything?"

"I did not!" he muttered, turning his eyes with a fixed stare at the well-scrubbed floor of the Council Chamber, yet not before letting me catch a glint of a severe eye and a tightening of lips which boded ill for my comfort when we should be alone that night."

"I hope," I said, turning to the political gentlemen, "that Doctor Pott and Senator Moll will pardon us "- ("Not 'us,'" groaned Dick -"and Ogord - you've made it worse - get on - oh, get on!") "I am a stranger," I added apologetically, "and a pilgrim - a pilgrim who has at last reached his Mecca - Cooktown!"

I thought that neat; so did the Cooktown Progress Association, and they signified their approval by staring at me sadly. Thus heartened, I lifted my eyes to the ceiling and addressed the few flies there with a long tirade on British cars.

I spoke of the hundreds of foreign cars which had attempted the Byerstown Range Road in vain (there was only one, but of course all other foreign aspirants would have failed; so it was rhetorical truth), and I tried to raise a vision for my audience of hundreds of magnificently painted, richly becushioned tin-cans with stream-lines containing meccano-set engines lying dead on that awful road; and I showed the simply built unpretentious little British car picking her way over their bones and bringing hope to Cooktown.

Dear Charles Petching said, "Hear, hear! " A big rosy-cheeked man near the back of the chamber gazed at me without any joy. He was, we learnt later, the agent for most of the cars north of Cairns - all, alas, foreign; and one could hardly expect him to appreciate oratorical flightiness which sent his products to the rubbish-heap. I lost him!

Then I went on to dilate on Dick's driving, suggesting very tactlessly that it was really very little in his life, and thereby losing the love of all the car-drivers in Cooktown, many of whom were present. I should add that from the moment of our arrival in Cooktown the womenfolk had been distinctly vocal on our performance, reasoning and talking as only women will reason and talk. "Ha!" they said in effect; "our motor-drivers - Ogord! they'd spend their time motoring round their verandas if they could get up the steps - *and they can't.*" Which, of course, was very unfair; the local men know that road; had we known it, we should never have attempted it.

Finally, and more happily, I suspect, for the Progress Association, I spoke as I felt of Cooktown's undoubted charm. Cooktown, when known, I said, and when the road had been repaired, would be a Mecca to all good Australians; in time - when the road was repaired - no Australian would rejoin mother earth without a Cooktown experience; tired Australians - when the road had been repaired - would come to Cooktown to rest; restless Australians would fly there (without bothering about roads, for Cooktown is potentially an excellent airport) to enjoy the wonderful sport, deep-sea fishing in the Great Barrier waters, warm delicious bathing, shooting crocodiles, kangaroos, dingoes, wild pigs, emu, wild geese, duck, and scrub and bush turkey; cold and rich Australians would rush over the repaired road in winter to warm up. And who, I begged, knows what it is to eat an orange until he has eaten a Cooktown sphere of golden sweetness and dropped its thin delicate skin-on the repaired road?

It was now that I lost Doctor Nott.

"What a beautiful harbour you have in Cooktown! This estuary of the Endeavour, sacred in its calm loveliness for all time as the place of refuge and hope, surely prepared for Captain Cook to careen his tight ship *Endeavour* in 1770. What can the other ports on the Queensland coast offer compared with Cooktown's commodious harbour? Townsville has a sewer, Cairns a great mud ditch and crocodile bath -"

"I congratulate these gentlemen on their wonderful motoring feat," said Doctor Nott a few minutes later, when I had sat down midst a deathlike silence punctuated with a few earnest little claps," but when 'Mr. MacPherson' talks of Townsville on a sewer and Cairns in a crocodile bath, I'm afraid I can't agree with him. And if I could," he added softly," it would be extremely injudicious of me to do so: both are in my constituency!"

I was covered with confusion, and seriously distressed. The Endeavour River mouth is worthy of all praise - usefully deep (when the channels are known), with quaint mountains to the northward surely placed there by the Superb Artist for His servant the sun to play on at sunset; but there was really no reason (beyond oratorical reason, which is a trifle unreasonable) to send the port of Cairns and the harbour at Townsville to muddy perdition while I raised the Endeavour to a turquoise pool fit for the angels.

I thought the meeting only partially successful, and the awful silence of Dick when we turned in that night was not encouraging. I looked forward to that day week, by which time the bad speech would be lived down.

Cooktown is truly in a shocking state. Most of the beer pumps (a sinister sign) are out of action in the vast hotels, many of which are slowly falling to ruin; one or two landladies persist in pumping tentatively, and I know of a good woman who keeps the wolf from the door of her inn and manages to bring up her small family by taking in plain sewing (rather against the nature of landladies, isn't it?) and trying her hand at hairdressing; but other elderly landladies, whose silk-covered breasts once shone bravely with heavy gold chains while their capable fingers held startling rings, are now glad to get the old-age pension. Three shops, rather decayed but still in use, in the main street were put up for auction during our visit and brought £13.10s. I spent more than an hour in the beautiful portentous-looking Queensland National Bank, and when the customer came in and banked £3 13s. 4d. he was received like a prince.

The cause of this effect is not far to find. Cooktown prepared to die when the great Palmer Goldfields were abandoned, and hope of partial resuscitation has faded with years of bad cattle seasons - drought and cattle-tick - while any hope of a useful tourist traffic developing must be put aside until the lovely little town is connected with the rest of Australia by motor road. This has killed the flourishing Cooktown of the eighties; but, judging on general principles, it is obvious to a stranger, if not to the present disheartened inhabitants who expect to be taking in one another's washing any day now, that the town will enjoy a resurrection. Harbours equalling the Endeavour are not plentiful on the northern Queensland coast; there is excellent fertile country in the neighbourhood capable of producing the best tropical fruit and vegetables in Australia, notably Cooktown oranges and the big clean peanuts which grow there; with capital, which will surely be attracted, thousands of square miles of extremely rich soil can be irrigated, for water is not scarce except in the form of rain; and there surely can be no reason why Cooktown should not again flourish on a better and more secure foundation than gold from the ground. As a matter of fact there is a very real danger threatening the town, although it will not be recognized as such; there seems a good chance of a revival of goldmining on the Palmer. More than fifty tons of gold were taken from the great dry river by the roughest and most old-fashioned methods; it is obvious that there must be infinitely more than that left. Already they have built a road from the Palmer to the Laura (connected with

Cooktown by railroad), and I suspect that after this wet season has passed great dredges will be working the pools where gold must have accumulated during count¬less ages. The great vaults of the Queensland National Bank should be in use once more. It will be a temporary wave of prosperity; let us hope that during its flood the townsfolk will realize that gold never yet built a permanent city, and that money will be earmarked for irrigation, road-making, and tilling the soil, for Cooktown's future lies along the hard yet wholesome road of serious tropical agriculture. Incidentally, I know of one farmer near Cooktown who, with the poorest means of transport and heavy freights south, clears £400 per annum from not a particularly large orange orchard.

I was very enthusiastic, and I fear officious, in urging the people to get the Byerstown Road repaired. "We," they said, "are always at the County Council!" "But," I said, "if the County Council won't move, and it probably hasn't enough money, why not start a road-making bee - make a picnic of it - take the girls out - *do it!*" Which was really very kind of me, considering that I would not be there myself to shoulder a pick !

The trouble with; Cooktown and the Cooktowners at the present moment is the entire lack of surprise in their mental atmosphere. Everyone knows that on Tuesday afternoon a launch will arrive from Cairns with a few passengers able to afford the expensive fare; everyone expects to see a red light shining from a local confectioner's and the notice" Ice-cream tonight!" (made from ice brought in the launch); but during the rest of the week nothing surprising happens, not even ice-cream. With a road through, all kinds of amusing and interesting folks will be dashing in and out of Cooktown; the distance from Cairns and the considerable towns on the Atherton Tablelands would be nothing with a good road; and - but it must be obvious to a man with half an eye!

We had a great time in Cooktown. Whenever a hostess asked us to a dance or to dinner she accompanied her invitation with a kind of trousseau: two each of her son's garments-two pairs of trousers, two shirts, two collars, two ties, and four collar studs. Mrs. Wallace of the Commercial Hotel always added two nicely ironed handkerchiefs. Without this kindly thought, we could not have accepted; all our party clothes were left in Cairns. Before we left the town, the elders of Cooktown presented us with a very fine address of appreciation and a considerable portion of the true old log which was once the true old tree to which Cook tied his *Endeavour* during his stay in 1770. But while there is much that I might write about Cooktown, I dare not; Cape York is still a long way ahead; but I can only be fair and I hope I may help Cooktown by saying that houses may be bought there very cheaply, that hotel accommodation is excellent, and that the climate between April and October is glorious and dry. I could imagine people with small incomes living very gracefully and happily in Cooktown; and the little town should make a fine centre for anyone interested in serious sport - crocodiles, pigs, kangaroos, etc.

Owing to the serious delay caused by the elders wanting us to meet Doctor Nott and Senator Foll, we decided to entrain the car to Laura, thus getting back to our route which we left to run into Cooktown from Butcher's Hill. Business does not now warrant the running of a locomotive ; the line is merely kept open by an old Napier automobile on steel wheels, just able to drag one small tender; but the short journey is wholly delightful. The station-master drives the motor, and the porter takes the tickets and puts the brakes on the tender going down steep pinches; everyone is friendly, even the few old men with long white whiskers who appear at the decayed stations on the way. For some reason the immense numbers of kangaroos, wallaroos, wallabies, pademelons and emus who inhabit the bush lining the track have a quaint desire to race the train. Disturbed by its approach, they begin a wild rush through the bush, tearing and bounding along and turning to leap magnificently across the line, sometimes a few feet in front of the motor. We saw some hundreds in a few hours.

Laura, or one should say *the* Laura - a local habit applied to all the small settlements - appears fresher than Cooktown because the Laura has now got down to bed-rock; all that can decay has decayed. There is a good railway station, one fine store, and an old inn shaded by mango-trees. The Laura is chiefly distinguished in my memory through its ant-castles, the most amazing erections I have ever seen. They are tall slabs of a shadowy green fabric rising up to fourteen feet and ending in a series of quaint little turrets. Very graceful, they are seldom more than eight or ten feet in length, with a base possibly two feet through. For some excellent reason, doubtless dependent on prevailing winds and best known to their clever little heads, the termites always build their amazing castles with the great flat sides facing exactly east and west, and the pointed ends to the north and south. A compass could not be more correct. It was fascinating to pass through many, many miles of country thickly covered with the tall green castles; and at sunset the sky-line they offered was weird; without any difficulty one could imagine oneself in some enchanted land occupied by artistic giants.

The Laura - and a glance at the map might be useful here - inland from Cooktown, marked our last certain centre for supplies; therefore it meant loading the car to the limit. We carried eight gallons of petrol on the back seat, two on the running-board, three quart bottles in the tuckerbox, and four in the tank. That, with our luggage made a very serious and dangerous load for the car on rough country. We knew that only the greatest care would see us through. Men we met at luncheon in the inn were greatly interested in our trip, for many of them had travelled up the Peninsula; but they were not seriously discouraging. Two or three of them thought the Jardine River would stop us, for, as they explained, the Jardine was wide, always running, and deep. But we felt that if we got as far as the Jardine, within thirty miles of Cape York, we could take the car to pieces if necessary and swim across a few hundred times. When we explained this, one man smiled. "There are - er - *lizards* in the Jardine! " he said. He meant crocodiles!

At the Laura we met some of the men engaged in building the road which will carry the dredging machinery to the Palmer; they were using a great six-wheeled British motor-lorry, which was giving magnificent service on the roughest work. The road had just been completed, and they all seemed very sanguine about the future.

We left the Laura at about two o'clock, and, following a faintly discernible bush road, we went gaily on our way, agreeably surprised when the road suddenly improved and permitted considerable speed. After a time, we saw, to our amazement, that another small car had left tracks. Then we noticed that at intervals a large shed, remarkably like a country grandstand, appeared! We were on a race-track, truly a bush race-track, for it simply made a great oval in the forest. We had gone round and round it; but we got out all right and pursued our way to Laura cattle-station, roughly eighteen miles to the north-east.

The road, the roughest of bush roads, had been traversed by cars and it was possible, very occasionally, to see that. it was a road, chiefly from the blazed trees! The grass on the actual road was three or four feet high at times, and we had to watch very carefully lest our axles should strike low ant-hills. However, we plugged gamely along without serious difficulty until we reached the crossing of the Laura River. Here we might have been held up some hours, if the manager of the cattle-station had not providentially appeared on his way up the river to the camp of his stockmen. His extra weight helped us through the very soft sand, and he sent us on our way rejoicing to his homestead a few miles farther on, promising to try and join us later.

The Laura cattle-station homestead is in a romantic clearing near the banks of the Laura River, which, like most of the major rivers of the Peninsula, is dry except during the wet season. However, by sinking a tank well down into the sand the Laura folks get enough water for cooking and household use. For drinking, they must depend on rainwater stored in immense tanks; during eight months there may be no rain. The house is built on tall piles, and the kitchen appears towards the rear of the great cool open space under the house. This space is the daily living-quarters of the family, who seldom mount the stairs to the rooms and balcony above, because they dislike being baked! Palms and ferns and a few pleasantly covered sofas here and there remove any harshness from the rough piles and beams. Good housewives have the ceiling scrubbed - and a difficult job it must be! - immediately after the upstairs rooms have been cleaned; otherwise there are soapy stalactites dangling along the beams. Charming spot, Laura homestead; the air is heavy with the scent of frangipani; there are plenty of orange and lime trees, banana palms, and other tropical shrubs and trees, fighting to live and give with the heavy disadvantage of long periods of drought each year. I might add here that, contrary to my own expectations, the vegetation in the Cape York Peninsula seldom appears tropically luxuriant. One passes through eucalyptus forest very similar to that found in New South Wales. There are differences, and there are even areas where the growth is rich and rank, but the country through which our trail passed was generally eucalyptus forest with little undergrowth.

At Laura homestead we found a very pleasant little woman with two beautiful little girls and a red-haired, wise young gentleman, aged seven, called Neil. There were two aboriginal girls employed in the kitchen, of excellent character and good workers, Mrs. Bell (our hostess) said. They are the wives of stockmen employed on the place, and their children play with the Bell kiddies on apparent terms of equality, and with just as much say in childish arguments. Neil was particularly fascinated by Laura, the cook's black baby of about eighteen months.

"I wonder," I said, "why she called the baby Laura? "

"Oh," said Neil, "because she found it under a tortoise shell on the bank of the Laura River. That's what she reckons," he added cautiously.

The children all appeared surprisingly healthy; this dry hot Queensland climate has apparently no malign effect on white children. Yet life would be full of anxiety for a less sensible woman than Mrs. Bell. There are many snakes of all varieties; pigs are almost as dangerous here as tigers are in other countries, a boar or a big sow being quite capable of killing and eating a child. Therefore the children keep within the homestead compound. But even here trouble came upon Neil when a big black snake bit him on the ankle a year ago. He tried to keep the matter dark, fearing to worry his mother, and he was furious when his sister "told on him" at once- thus saving his life. For Mrs. Bell immediately obeyed directions, cutting the boy's ankle between the punctures, pushing in "Condy's," and fitting a ligature. Then she took him to the doctor - that is, she rode sixteen miles to the Laura and fortunately found a train ready to start for Cooktown ; if the train had not been ready, she would have had to wait a week!

Mrs. Bell has not been long out from England, and all her relations live at home. She was neither enthusiastic nor otherwise about life in the Never Never, apparently accepting it as a normal enough existence, keeping her home rigidly clean, and bringing up her children in what I, as a bachelor, thought very much the right way. I felt, when they all trooped upstairs, leaving us to cool stretchers "under the house," in a sweet atmosphere of cool ferns and distant frangipani, that we had all been to a very nice children's party.

We left Laura Station at 7.30 the next morning, and immediately entered an enchanted wood. The forest on each side of the trail was literally alive with game, not seriously disturbed by the car's approach - all kinds of kangaroo, emu, opossum, iguana (some very large fellows), and pigs. We never killed for the fun of killing; but we had no conscience qualms in shooting what pigs we could; they are a great pest. Once we saw an immense boar trotting off, and he was hardly smaller than a St. Bernard dog. As we progressed, great lagoons became more plentiful. They were beautiful lagoons bearing multi-coloured lotus and water-lily blossoms on their shimmering surface. A sportsman with one poor eye could have filled his bag ten times - duck of all kinds, pelican, native companion, and vast flocks of wild geese. When we fired and killed a goose for the pot, the noise made by the goose's escaping mates was almost deafening.

We crossed the Kennedy River after much difficulty, and noon found us resting on the banks of what seemed a wide river of cool clear water, not, however, running. With a little more energy we should both have plunged in, for this water looked so perfectly harmless, and our hours of navvying had made us rather unclean. Had we done so, these words could not have been written. We should have lived but a few minutes; the Kennedy Bend is notorious even in this crocodile-infested area for its special breed of vicious reptiles. The Kennedy Bend is a kind of parking area for crocodiles during the "dry." I often think with a shudder of that long pool; and, as it is, I know that we narrowly missed being swept in by a mighty tail as we stood on the edge of the deep water dropping crumbs to small fish.

It was a lovely and interesting trail we followed that day for over forty miles, and we hope to return there one day to spend a few weeks shooting pigs and crocodiles. Towards the late afternoon we reached the gates of Lakefield cattle-station.

It should amuse Australian folks in particular to know how we approached the manager or owner of a cattle-station. The only way, and the accepted way, is to blow up to the homestead, shake hands and say, "How d'ye do! " and take up your residence; but even at the very end of our Journey we could never feel very happy about doing that. In our inmost hearts we really longed for a comfortable bed and food from a table; but we invariably said, "D'you know of a good camping-ground near here - with water handy?" We were always given directions, and rather apologetically we would accept tea or refreshment of some kind, "I'm afraid we're giving you a lot of trouble-" sort of thing. Then our host or hostess would say, "But surely - surely, you'll spend at least the night with us?" We would then say we would - and " thanks very much!"

However, I'm not convinced that people in the Never-Never are always wildly excited with joy when a stranger appears to live on them. It is amazing the number of inconsequential people who roam about the outposts of a country. If the stranger is amusing and interesting, he is welcome, as he is welcome in a city home-but he gives extra work; if he is dull and boring, he not only gives extra work, but the pain he inflicts is just as real in the backblocks as it is in the town. I know one large station where the family is seldom alone. When the strangers who are always drifting to the homestead eventually depart with conventional thanks and the hostess says, "Oh delighted!" they often reply pityingly, " Yes - it must be wonderful for you to see fresh faces - good-bye!" The poor woman then rushes to make up beds in the guest rooms for the next lot!

I suspect that Mr. MacDowell, the manager of Lakefield, leads the most exciting life lived in Australia. If he went about his place unarmed, there would very shortly be no Mr. MacDowell. One day he wounded a large boar, which instantly charged him. He was mounted, and might have got away if his horse had not ,been held up by some thick scrub. The boar leapt to rip the belly of the horse. Fortunately the horse swerved. The pig clipped off eight joints of the horse's tail!

Obviously there was no scrub too thick to hold up the horse after that little amputation! We saw the tail, kept at the homestead as a souvenir. My own impression is that the boar only clipped off five joints (concurrently, of course), but Dick insists on eight. I cannot tell; and I offer this doubt because a man on Thursday Island asserted that a horse has only eight joints altogether in his tail. Certainly it was only half a tail we inspected.

Mr. MacDowell has a lot to do with crocodiles.

One day he had mustered a dozen weaners, leaving them together near a bend in a river or long pool while he went to collect more. Twenty minutes later he heard a soul-stirring bellowing, and, suspecting crocodiles, he rode quickly back to the weaners. One was missing. Very quietly he stole over to a deep pool of water, and in this he watched an immense crocodile holding the young bullock in its jaws, waving it to and fro in the water, drowning it, of course, before towing it off to the alligatorial kitchen where food is kept until it gets "high." A few shots from his revolver and much whip-cracking induced the crocodile to make off. The weaner was dragged up on to the bank and left there, while the men returned to the homestead (quite near) for poison. They were convinced that the crocodile had had the fright of his life and would not return for some hours; but when they returned an hour later the weaner had disappeared. Unpleasant beasts; one never takes water from suspected lagoons or river pools without precautions. One of the simplest is to fill the billy near lotus or water-lily plants, keeping an eye on the floating leaves. Despite his immense size, a crocodile on the hunt makes no sound and little apparent movement in the water; but he is thwarted by the water-lilies, whose leaves and flowers rise and fall as his long thick body glides past their sensitive spirals.

These lagoons offer plenty of fish, chiefly barramundi, which is easily caught with live bait. But, frankly, we had no time for serious fishing or hunting; we caught and shot merely what we needed for the pot, and the pot was nearly always full.

We were very kindly treated by Mr. and Mrs. MacDowell. Mr. MacDowell is rather like Tom Mix. The homestead is a very pleasant bungalow, and it was here that we learned the necessity of scrubbing the ceiling of the "under the house." It had the effect of making us examine the ceiling of all the other houses we entered. The MacDowells employ aboriginal labour, and successfully, I gathered. There was one intelligent little black boy employed in the kitchen garden. I asked for his name, expecting to hear something with an interesting sound in his own language. "My name's Hector!" said he with a very proud, slightly defiant look. "So's mine! " I said.

We had been told as far south as Brisbane of a Presbyterian missionary who had driven his car from Laura to Weipa. Weipa is near Albatross Bay on the north-west coast of the Peninsula. He had shipped his car from Cairns to Cooktown by steamer, and by rail from Cooktown to Laura. We heard definite news of his adventure at Lakefield. We had imagined something ascetic in an old Ford; Mr. MacDowell told us of one in a large new American car with a charming wife and a small daughter - a determined exciting character, very far removed from the pale worthy creature of our imaginings. We met him eventually; but as we followed his trail for a time, we often talked of him, calling him the Flying Missionary.

It seems that he had spent a day or two with the MacDowells overhauling his car and resting. He left one morning early with great eclat, tooting his horn most musically while his good wife waved to her hostess. The road is hardly more than a series of cattle-pads, littered with fallen timber and dotted about with low ant-heaps as hard as cement. But the Flying Missionary took off and flew down the slope swiftly, and before turning a bend he made even more music, while his wife shouted, "Good-bye, Mrs. MacDowell - good-bye-ee!"

Alas, a few minutes later came more music from the horn, but now of a melancholy nature. The MacDowells instantly read S.O.S., and went to the rescue. They found the missionary standing before his car waving a chunk of hardwood in his hand.

"This is only half of the stump I hit, Mr. MacDowell," he called; "the other half's in my bonnet!"

Well, it was bigger than a bee, and some days were spent in repairing the car. Eventually the missionary again took off, and Mr. MacDowell heard nothing more of him. We did. Indeed, when we met him, we felt we had known him all our lives.

We had hoped to leave Lakefield soon after dawn, but we found the car with both back tyres punctured, and it meant getting to work to mend them. Perhaps our tyre-covers were a trifle tight; at any rate the removal of the covers was only a little less difficult than putting them back. The tyre-levers we had bought in Sydney bent like dough; screwdrivers and file ends of course made fresh punctures if great care were not taken. It sometimes took more than half an hour to get a tyre-cover off, and more than that to get it on. Imagine our language when, upon blowing it up, we found, as we sometimes did, that the screw-driver or the file end had made a fresh hole!

Hence it was that ten o'clock had struck in the Lakefield homestead before at last we got away. That meant travelling during the worst part of the day, navvying our way across creeks and watercourses in great heat, with flies driving us mad. Fortunately for us, a Lands Commissioner had motored from Lakefield to the Stewart River two months earlier. He had native help, and we found the river crossings prepared. The tracks of his car were as plain as if he had passed a few hours before us. He was the third car to get as far north as we were then; we were the fourth. In time, of course, we left them all behind.

North of Lakefield we came across our first devil-devil country and sand-ridges. Mrs. MacDowell had warned us about the latter, but I thought she had said "sandwiches," and I expected something unusual and terrifying. But sand-ridges are simply long mounds of sand hardly apparent in that bush-covered country; they did not annoy us. The devils did, however. Devil-devil country was well up to Constable Pitchern's estimate. Devil-devil occurs on great infertile flats subject to yearly flooding; if wet, it would not be difficult to sink from sight in it. The roots and stems of reeds and other low stunted growth apparently hold up the rubbish which is being swept slowly across the flat by the flood water. Sand and mud join the compote, and the end of the flood sees a close succession of hard little mounts rising from a few inches to as high as two feet. Each little mount, a kind of porcupine mole-hill, is hard, and a car is tortured as she plugs along with each wheel at a different level. Occasionally the under-gear of the car is gripped by inconveniently arranged devils, and then it means much work carving them down.

Fortunately the devil-devil country appeared in patches, not often more than a mile in width; no rain came; we had no need to stop for fear of falling into the bosom of Australia; and we managed the devils very well. Otherwise the going was not at all bad.

The end of the day saw us driving cheerfully down a slope through a forest of very tall, thin, exactly perpendicular gum-trees. The sun was setting on our left, creating in that forest a curious mauve haze. Ants had plastered all the tall slim gum-trees with covered ways of mud all the way up to the branches. The soil on the slope must have been of different colours; much of it had been burnt red with bush-fires of the past; near newly-burnt logs it was black and brown. The ants had taken the soil nearest to hand, and the truly lovely result in that mauve haze was a succession of straight lines of red, pink, black white and brown. The effect was startling in its beauty.

Just before we reached the bottom of this gentle slope we heard shouts: "Stop-stop!" And we stopped. We heard cow-bells jangling, and soon we were able to see a few dozen horses making off for their lives, but seriously deterred by hobbles. I noticed that, while the horses were very frightened, they were also very curious. They could not resist the temptation to pause occasionally and look round at us with their ears sharply pricked.

When calm had been restored, we motored slowly down to a great bark shelter to greet the mailman. He pauses at this camp called the Eighteen Mile only once in every fourteen days; we were lucky to strike him. He was a very kind and courteous little man, and offered us a share of his provisions, although he had merely enough to take him through to the Laura. Fortunately we had no need to accept his hospitality.

Travelling with him was a young man called Henry, suffering with violent toothache, and on his way to the dentist. The journey was apparently occupying two or three weeks. However, Henry and his tooth, and the Eighteen Mile, demand a new chapter.

9

Henry's Tooth

I HOPE Henry will forgive me if I grind out a moral with that annoying molar of his. While I chatted with him in the leaping shadows of the great bark shelter with the glowing fire at its end, whereon danced large billies of salt beef and sweet potatoes, I felt for him, understanding, I think, just how boring and hopeless life seemed.

He seldom, if ever, sees a girl; and I'm certain he would like to see one occasionally, even if it were only once a month. I guessed that. And I think it is particularly hard for Henry, because, when once a year he joins the giddy whirl at Cooktown for the annual show, he is the hero of the race-track, the slim handsome knight of the Never-Never, and the girl he chooses is envied by all the others. But when the show is over, back he must ride to the depths of the great Peninsula to be lost and wasted. And Henry knows they are always having jazz-parties in Cooktown; he knows, as he turns in each night in that lonely little iron cottage on his cattle-station, that "the only girl" (if there is one) is dancing to the strains of the Commercial Hotel gramophone, twining like ivy about the miserable carcase of some Bill Smith or Tommy Grant - mere rats of men, who could not sit for more than a second on Henry's waler.

The journey to Cooktown is bad enough, even if it occupies less than a week; but if Henry decides to go south, say to Cairns, the business assumes the proportions of an expedition. He must travel by the S.S. *Kalatina*.

The *Kalatina* is more inconstant than the moon; she is an old steamer of some seven hundred tons, concerned chiefly in feeding the Peninsula coast, especially on the Gulf of Carpentaria side; she is quite unable to keep a time-table, and without wireless she cannot even let the telegraph people at Coen know when she may be expected at Port Stewart. However, she appears off the small Flinders Group about once every five weeks, and, when the man on Flinders sees her smoke, he mans the tender and wanders up the muddy mouth of the Stewart River to the rotting wharf, the shed, the old deserted humpy, and the great herd of white goats, which together make up Port Stewart. No one seems to live at Port Stewart, now.

If Henry is travelling by the *Kalatina*, he must be at Port Stewart a few days before the steamer's expected arrival; and he may wait fourteen days. I know of two innocent women who had to wait more than a month, but the circumstances were exceptional. The *Kalatina* had been seduced into tendering the Japanese liner *Tango Maru*, which sat on a spiked rock off Thursday Island. The profits were great, so we must not blame the *Kalatina*. At Port Stewart Henry will have company. Mr. Armbruist, the storekeeper from Coen, forty miles back, will be there with his team; and there may be some other whites. Once on the *Kalatina*, Henry begins the rush of modern life, and a few days will see him in Cairns.

The *Kalatina* is not an ocean greyhound, nor does she look very attractive; but actually her accommodation is not uncomfortable, and the food on board is extremely good. She is of great importance in the Peninsula; time and events are reckoned according to her movements. "Old Smith died," a Peninsula man might say, "well, let me see - ah, yes, it was just after the *Kalatina* before last."

I may be giving the impression that this neighbourhood is seriously populated. It is not, of course; including missionaries on the west coast, I should imagine fifty would be an optimistic estimate of the population in a country with an area as great as England.

I could see nothing attractive in life as it is lived here. I thought food the greatest drawback, as it always is far away from towns. Often on a cattle-station where there are perhaps thousands of cows they use condensed milk; meat will not keep more than a day; it is not often convenient to make yeast bread, and so damper suffices; there seems little tropical fruit beyond mangoes, and green vegetables are not always grown. The result is obvious. A bushman from the neighbourhood of Darwin told me that bush hotels keep a supply of soda tablets in their bars.

I used to enjoy books on the Wild West - Zane Grey and others; but since our trek north I am always searching through their pages to get some information about the food the characters live on. I notice that Zane Grey and the others seldom if ever feed them. I suppose they daren't. If it were explained that these bright-eyed, muscular, quick-drawing heroic outlaws had fierce-looking salt beef and gross sweet potatoes for breakfast, varied by salt beef and sweet potatoes for dinner, with something by way of a change to salt beef and sweet potatoes for supper, together with damper and black, heavily besweetened tea, we should instantly know that our heroes had chronic indigestion and carried peptones in their wallets. Thus would romance die! Lasca (down by the Rio Grande) ate salt beef and damper, I'll swear; and it is more than likely that her virile lovers had a touch of heart-burn, as well as the other thing. And it would be condensed milk or nothing for Lasca. It is not recorded that any of her lovers thought of roping the maiden a dairy cow from the range. I suspect that all this desperate shooting and murdering that occurs in the Wild West may be traced to indigestion and bad livers.

I am, of course, trying to be amusing; but nevertheless the subject has a serious aspect and demands careful research. Thousands of pounds are spent yearly in preparing live stock for the various agricultural shows throughout Australia; magnificent beasts in superb condition march pridefully past the judge; but I wonder if he ever gives a thought to the sallow-skinned human beast who occasionally leads the cattle. There is every chance of seeing a physically fit bull led by a man with false teeth who takes peptones. What, I ask, does it profit a man if he spends thirty years in producing an exquisite herd of Jersey cows and finds his daughter with a hare-lip? In a more enlightened age we shall find Australian pastoralists "showing" their employees, and it will be more glorious to boast of a dozen physically perfect champion and first prize stockmen than that number of champion Hereford bulls. I can see farmers of the future working out the diet of their men as today they work out the feeding of their bulls and rams, giving grave attention to teeth, sleeping-quarters, and healthy amusement; and then we shall find many, many more young fellows going back to the land in Australia instead of mooching about the cities, where it must be admitted, they enjoy better health than their brothers in the country, who, unless they are the sons of rich landholders, are not characterized by glowing health mentally or spiritually. Feed cattle unintelligently, and they'll throw runts; live yourself on salt beef and sweet potatoes, or even without plenty of fresh vegetables, and you'll do likewise.

To return to Henry and his wisdom tooth! When we met him he was travelling to the Laura with the mailman; it was then Friday; he had been riding for about two days, and I heard the mailman express the confident hope that he would catch the mail motor-train the following Tuesday or

Wednesday. We heard later on Thursday Island - Henry's tooth was quite famous in the land - that he eventually reached Cairns, where, in pulling out the tooth, they broke his jaw. Which may explain why it had resisted all efforts with bits of string and slamming doors, also the pliers and pincers of helpful friends, black and white, in the neighbourhood.

Well, it may not have been so bad for Henry; let's hope that during the period of convalescence he met a pleasant nurse or a pretty probationer deeply interested in the repair of his jaw.

We all slept in the long *gunyah* near the pools of discoloured water (the reason for the mail¬change here). Henry, poor man, was obviously having a bad time with his molar; Dick, near me, went "right out"; the mailman, surrounded by his pack-saddles of precious mail, slept; but great fatigue, some anxiety regarding the road ahead of us, and the romance in our situation, kept me awake most of the night.

Just before dawn I saw a dim figure approach the dead or dying fire at the end of the long shelter, and within a few seconds the place was alive with dancing shadows. The mailman and Henry instantly rose and began the business of their day; Dick and I bathed in one of the less discoloured pools a little distant from the camp (a luxury we could not forgo), and, while he attended to the punctures which we could not repair the night before, I got breakfast.

A black was busy making johnny-cakes, carefully kneading the snowy dough with his long, black, graceful fingers, and flopping the flat cakes efficiently on the hot. grey ash at the edge of the fire. Here they rose in tiny mountains and were turned at precisely the right moment. Sweet potatoes were being warmed, and the hunks of salt beef in the large billies of rich brown water (like varnish in colour) began dancing as gaily as they had danced the night before.

Our breakfast consisted of oatcakes and butter with stewed apples and tea. The menu was obviously simple, but quite adequate. My mother used to make oatcakes, and I've tramped many happy miles in the Highlands with a packet of oatcakes in my pocket. Their preparation is simple, and I think they cannot be beaten on an expedition. The absence of soda in their composition allows the oatmeal to remain completely nutritious. I might offer a bush recipe, although I am certain that more than one Scotch body will up and put me right. "Soul," of course, is necessary for the making of good oatcakes, as it is necessary in the making of a bed. However - rub, say, a little more than a tablespoonful of butter (or good dripping if butter is not about) into a cup of honest oatmeal, adding a pinch of salt; achieve a thick sticky kind of dough by adding not too much very hot water; flatten out into fairly thin cakes, and place on a piece of tin (in the absence of a good iron girdle) over a not too fierce fire. If the fire is too hot, the cakes will burn, and the inside will not be cooked. When cooked, the cakes are soft, but if they are placed near the fire (like toast waiting for breakfast) they harden up, and may be kept to be eaten at odd times. Damper may wreck weak" innards; oatcakes will not.

Incidentally we failed to obtain anywhere in Queensland those big square ships' biscuits; in my opinion they come next to oatcakes for rough work.

After the Eighteen Mile the way improved considerably. There were sand-ridges and a spot of devil-devil, but we made good progress. We were seldom held up for long at the creeks and watercourses, the crossings of which had all been made ready by that excellent Lands Commissioner. Towards noon we reached a cattle-station homestead called Lotusvale. The owner was unfortunately absent, but the manager, Felix Harvey, did the honours of host very effectively. Felix must be nearly fifty. He was born in the Peninsula and has apparently never been out of it - never farther south than Cairns. He was a fount of information. He had the same musical, rather blase-sounding accent that our friend Roy has. His opinion of town-dwellers was not very high ; and one can hardly blame him. His love of a certain sanguinary adjective spoken more often than printed was most exciting. We were bound to admit an astounding efficiency in its use. For instance, if he left out one before even a humble noun, and occasionally between syllables, he began the sentence again and put it in. I shall use dashes; they are inadequate; but bad people (if any) may have some fun translating the dashes and saying over Felix's speeches. They must be said with gathering speed and with great force at the end.

" A -- man has to be -- careful with - city -- blokes. I've never been south of -- Cairns. I s'pose if a -- man went south of -- Cairns with any -- money in his -¬pockets, they'd take his -- money, cut his -- throat, and throw his -- body in the -- river!"

Felix got great emphasis on that "-- river !" slowing up a trifle.

"I've got -- whiskers now" - feeling his hairy chin -"it's because I've got a sore -- skin. But when I see -- hair on a -- man's -- face, I -- well know there's -- dirt behind it! A -- man came south here from -- Cape York with -- hair all over his -- face. I said, 'Here's a -- pair of -- scissors; cut it off !' He said, 'Take your -- scissors away!' And," said Felix knowingly, "he was arrested at the -- Laura for -- murder! "

Obviously, a man hiding from the law with a beard!

We should have liked to spend more time with Felix, but time was now very important. The weather looked promising, but we never knew when it would change. We were actually beginning a dash to Cape York, now roughly four hundred miles to the north of us. Therefore, after an excellent dinner, we bade Felix goodbye and pushed on our way. After a good run of thirty miles we reached Running Creek.

The name is completely distinctive in the neighbourhood. It is the only creek with good running water within hundreds of miles. Certainly we saw no more honest running water until we reached the Batavia River at Moreton telegraph station. The creek runs in a very deep valley, and its clear cool water is most attractive to fatigued dirty travellers. Still, I was not entirely comfortable sitting in a pool that evening doing the family washing. I kept the electric torch on, and when two socks, each from a pair and very good ones too, escaped and ran merrily down the creek into a deep-looking pool, I did not follow them. Local men will laugh if crocodiles are feared in Running Creek; but the neighbourhood is distinctly crocodile country, and I felt that one possibly might have decided to have a look around Running Creek that night.

We were now travelling north-east, actually making for the neighbourhood of Port Stewart, called Moojeeba on the map and a little north of Princess Charlotte Bay. The McIlwraith Range had to be crossed, and it seemed best to cross it on the wagon road from Port Stewart to the Coen (a small inland settlement). We were now passing up the coast, a score of miles inland, and we had reached the neighbourhood of the Balclutha River. We were still following the very helpful tracks left by the Lands Commissioner; occasionally we heard of the Flying Missionary.

We had left Running Creek betimes in the morning, and noon found us being very pleasantly entertained by Herbert Thompson of Silver

Plains at a camp by the way, where he was collecting cattle and de-horning bulls. A magnificently built man of about forty-five, I should judge, he was deeply interested in his vast station and cattle, but life in the wild had not destroyed a very pretty sense of humour which pervaded his conversation and kept us amused during every minute of our stay with him. He had his son with him and a few native stockmen. When he sells cattle, he must drive them to Mareeba; and this occupies roughly six weeks. Obviously, when he reaches Mareeba he is not in a good position to argue about prices; the dealers know he will shrink from driving them all the way back! He told us that if the cattle were efficiently driven south and not pushed, they put on flesh during the journey, for much of the country on the way, just after or even during the "wet," offered magnificent fodder. We had dinner together under a canvas shelter, and, when it was time to push on, young Thompson went with us a mile along the track, guiding us to a great lagoon, upon which sat, I should imagine, ten thousand wild geese and thousands of duck of all varieties. We shot a fat young goose and hurried on to a tidal creek passable only at low and half-tide. This was an unsavoury business - filthy muddy platforms of rock with biggish pools on each side of us - but we found no serious difficulty, and by three o'clock we had reached the near bank of the Stewart River. Here, alas, the car tracks left by the Lands Commissioner ended. Not having much business to attend to farther north, he had shrunk from the Stewart.

The river looked very bad - a great wide gulley of soft white sand with deep pools occurring along the near side - but we had to tackle it. Having dropped down the near bank, we paused in the bed and worked opt plans. The sand, we now saw, rose gently to the far side, often forming soft banks. On the other hand, the sand near the pools was firm on the surface, but possibly quick. We decided to rush at great speed along this dampish sand and then to make a quick swerve at a point where the sandbanks were fewer and where the river narrowed. The climb of the far bank had to be considered, for this was a low rocky ledge, which we saw demanded much work. Although occasionally that firm damp sand shook and waved, it stood up to the car's weight; we got up great speed, and the swerve took us to within a few yards of the far bank. As very good luck would have it, an old native with long whiskers came rushing down to us, followed by a black woman - natives employed at Silver Plains homestead on the far bank of the Stewart - and together we soon had the car free of the river.

The poor Flying Missionary in his rich American car had had less success. He attempted the river some miles farther east, where it is tidal. The sand was firmer to begin with, but the river is four or five times wider. Half-way across he stuck, and there seemed no way out of his difficulty. Then the tide came in. When a gentle little wave lapped his wheels he knew it was time to retreat. The car was abandoned to the sea, and the missionary, with his wife and child, followed by his native servant, began the long walk across the sandy river to the far bank. They were greatly distressed at losing their car, but a fresh danger now arose. The sand was becoming remarkably like quicksand as the tide came in; and darkness fell. However, they reached the far bank and found the road from Port Stewart to Herbert Thompson's homestead. Here they were very kindly treated and spent the evening bewailing their loss.

The next morning the Flying Missionary led an expedition to the wreck. To his amazement the car was discovered in perfect condition; the gentle little wave which had lapped his wheels was actually one of the last efforts of the incoming tide.

Forty blacks were collected, and these were placed on a long rope ready to pull when the engine should start. The natives had the rope good and taut, and to encourage them the missionary gave a violent honk to his horn. The natives instantly dropped the rope and made off. Herbert Thompson mustered them again, and once more they were ready to pull, but by an unfortunate combination of circumstances the car back-fired like a cannon-shot at the same moment that the clutch engaged with a soul-stirring rattle - and it is said that the natives are going yet ! The missionary then put his gears in reverse and the car rushed beautifully back to the south bank. He had better success farther up the river.

We motored to the gates of Silver Plains homestead and found there two native women left in the stern charge of the old fellow who had helped us up the river-bank. As a chaperon he appeared inadequate. The young women spent their time laughing at him, calling him "the ole man," ordering him about most peremptorily, and finally chasing him up the mango-trees to find ripe mangoes for us. Presumably he would report any irregularity to the husbands - stockmen at Herbert Thompson's camp - but I doubt if he could, or would, do battle with any dark-skinned lovers.

Naturally I do not want to gossip about the aboriginal women; I always feel that native races under the critical eye of travellers and explorers have as much privacy as a gold-fish; but, according to reports, I fear it is not possible to give them full marks for either restraint or serious resistance to the blandishments of their male friends. An attempt is made by their protectors to keep them virtuous, but this is only partially successful. There is a regulation in the North apparently encouraging the employers of native women to lock them up each night, and to this the dark maidens submit quite cheerfully, notably when they can arrange to have a sweetheart hidden behind a curtain or under the bed - and locked up with them! Aboriginal cooks and maids appear so serious and stern that it seems difficult to imagine them being wicked.

Dear good Mrs. S., of a certain mission, loved her girls in the young women's dormitory with an affection so trusting that it became almost belligerent when she met others more experienced and less enthusiastic.

"I," she used to say, "find my young women and girls splendid. Yes, I lock them up most carefully at seven and count them; but only because of this absurd regulation."

That, however, was some years ago. Mrs. S's love for her charges had not weakened - indeed it had strengthened with the years - but her attitude had changed. When with all possible delicacy we reminded her of a slightly comic incident of which we had heard (I think it was a compliment to Mrs. S. that we could do so), she wagged a finger at us and said, "You naughty boys - who told you that?" Needless to say we did not tell her.

"Can you imagine what I felt? "she went on, with a woeful expression belied by a touch of mischief in dark bright eyes; "I was new at mission work - just up from the South, from a country parish -!"

"It must have been a bit startling for you," I offered.

"I wanted," said the good lady, "to cry - and then to take a stick to the lot of them!

" Yes," she admitted, " the story is quite true; boards in the young women's dormitory floor had been loose for months! And, "she added with a delicious drooping at the corners of her mouth, "those that came in were not all girls. But," said Mrs. S., closing the subject; "I think I *understand* now. I also inspect the floorboards occasionally!"

The natives at Silver Plains that day were wound up with excitement at our visit, and each of the three showed us his tricks. The old fellow was hopping about on one leg at a time, brandishing his long pole, but totally unable to concentrate on the job of knocking down what few ripe man-goes there were on the lovely trees. I. began to climb a tree myself, but one of the women shrieked, "Green ants," and so I gave it up. Green ants are hardly half an inch long, but they are packed tight with courage. The moment they smell a human's approach, they prepare to attack. They will run up under trousers, down necks, and up sleeves. Then they bury their little beaks deep into skin and wave their abdomens on high while they bite furiously. They seem to exude some sticky substance to help them along. This is more unpleasant than the actual bite, which is not very painful. Faced with certain death, they will yet bite. A green ant which has dropped from a tree into a car (quite by mistake), where he must know by the unusual surroundings and awful smells that he cannot live, will instantly bite. They live largely in trees, where they make excellent little houses by gumming leaves together. No one camps near them. They are carnivorous, apparently. I have watched them waiting near pools for small black ants. A green ant will grab his victim in his jaws and then transfer it to one of his forefeet and begin his march home with his mouth on the defensive. For on the journey he may have fifty fights with other green ants. I have heard of a pitched battle between the much bigger meat-ants and the green fellows. The result was something of a draw; but no green corpses were captured by the meat-ants. Each side carried its own dead home to the larder.

One of the native women at Silver Plains, a little older than the other, sat on a rocking-chair with her hastily donned "mother-hubbard" decorously covering her thin black legs. (Native women have legs like sticks.) As she rocked, with a proud little smile on her thin lips, she kept up a running conversation in a thin treble voice. She was letting us and her mates appreciate her English vocabulary. Much of it escaped me. It was distinctly like a little girl repeating very nicely, "The cat is on the mat. The cat caught a rat. The rat is dead!"

"Jinny's man," I heard her say once; pointing to her friend, who was bullying the "ole man" and driving him back to the mango-tree, Jinny's man - oh, him he big feller: Billy! You see Billy - with Boss?"

We said that we had. Followed a few more rockings, a few more pleasant little smiles, and then the proud boast:

"Sometimes, I make damper (bread) for Boss!" We congratulated her with an encouraging "Well, well - good girl, what!" and she continued happily and innocently:

"Boss, very sick one time; close-up him he die - finish."

It was, of course, extremely rude of me; but I couldn't resist the temptation to ask, " Was that after the damper, Mary?" I expected her to laugh; I was not prepared for the rest of the story.

"Yessir!" she said; "Boss and young Boss come home too much tired at night. Boss say, 'I too dead tired to makem damper.' Young Boss say, 'Me too!' Boss say, 'Get Mary makem damper!' So I make damper for Boss."

Mary was tremendously proud.

"Boss and young Boss eatem that damper - they likem too much. Bimeby Boss say while he sit on chair -'Oh my gord!' Then he get plenty sick - and close-up him he die. Young Boss give him salt medcin."

"If that Jinny and the other woman ask you for flour or tea - don't you give 'em any!" had warned young Thompson; "we left them plenty, and I'll bet they say they have none; they'll have sold it for tobacco."

He was right. The "ole man," Jinny, and Mary, were enduring so awful a tea and flour famine that, had we remained the night at Silver Plains, we should have been similarly stricken. We therefore made a contribution, but chiefly of tobacco, and passed on our ways.

After a quick run; to Port Stewart, and finding nothing there more exciting than the rickety wharf, the old shed, and the tumbledown house with the few hundred white goats around it, we returned past Silver Plains and on towards Coen.

The road from Silver Plains to the foot of the McIlwraith Range is a magnificent boulevard compared with that south of the Stewart, but its twenty odd miles occupied the remaining four hours of daylight. Darkness found us staring hopelessly at a cutting of one sheer rise pointing at the stars. Had we been able to take a "run" at it on second, with something up our sleeves in the way of first, conceivably we might have managed it. But that abomination of hard sandstone, thickly dusted with soft white loose sand, began with a creek! Therefore the poor little car had to begin on low, Dick driving, while I pushed and chocked with stones when necessary.

Hours passed. We were half-way up, and the road had offered rest in a short stretch of level before beginning something positively unbelievable. We were hungry; we were utterly exhausted, but we stuck to it. It must have been past midnight when we reached the point where the road turns to the final rise. But this was beyond us that night; we could do no more.

We had little water, and we were filthy; we were hungry, and for a time too exhausted to prepare food. Finally we struggled towards that fat young goose hanging from the hood; with gathering interest we plucked and cleaned it, and, in short, we eventually ate fat tender portions of it stewed in boiling dripping. I stuffed the remainder of the main carcase with chopped-up onions and mangoes, leaving it in a biscuit-tin covered with slightly bad butter to roast slowly and gracefully during the night in the ashes of the camp-fire.

In the morning we used block and tackle, Dick driving, while I pulled; and after much hard work in great heat, with small flies again driving us frantic, we reached a ridge of the range. I confess I urged an immediate spell, but Dick has a violent habit of persisting in finishing the matter in hand before resting, and so we began the tiresome task of carrying up the baggage and petrol which we had been forced to leave half-way up the hill.

A most unpleasant bit of road, that Coen hill; we had been told that sixteen horses are required to drag the storekeeper's wagon up its steep length. Indeed, more than once I feared we would have to walk to Coen to get help. But, safely at the top, we decided that if anyone asked us about it, we would say with raised eyebrows and a surprised expression, "A hill - a steep pinch! Is there one?"

After filling the radiator, our supply of water was reduced to about half a pint. We had not been able to wash that morning, and as we drove along that rough road we felt very uncomfortable and rather peevish, Somewhere about eleven o'clock we saw white buildings across a low valley, and we halted beneath the shade of a large gum-tree. Here we ate the pleasant relics of the cold roast goose, and having washed, shaved, and brushed our teeth (on the half-pint of water), we swept into Coen and drew up at the hotel.

Hiding much interest and some excitement beneath a perfectly nonchalant if hospitable expression, the hotel-keeper, Mr. Armbruist, welcomed us.

"Well," said he with a chuckle; " how did you manage - the pinch?"

Dick glanced at me with a puzzled expression which I returned.

"The pinch? " I inquired.

"That steep bit - where you get up from the plains?" he encouraged.

"Is there a steep bit? " I asked; "we thought the road rather level - bumpy, perhaps, but nothing exceptional."

"Oh well," said Mr. Armbruist, "perhaps you and Sir Charles will come in and have a drink. You can put the aeroplane in the chicken-house later."

Coen must have been a delightful town to live in before the high cost of labour forced the gold-mines in the neighbouring mountains to close. Its situation could hardly be bettered for an inland town - a fine view of mountains and valleys stretching to the plain lands of the west, a fertile soil which produces excellent vegetables and flowers, and an adequate supply of water from the Coen River, which, while apparently dry, has a sand so wet that tubs and tins can be filled in no time if they are sunk a little. There is, too, a running creek. There were two hotels at one time, even a chemist's shop and plenty of stores. The town was well designed, I guessed, with streets surrounding a square.

I fear today it has to be a guess, for Coen is slowly dying. Indeed, when we were there, a crisis was imminent. Mr. Armbruist runs the hotel, but I can hardly believe the yearly profits in the bar meet the licensing fee, and guests like ourselves appear but seldom. He owns cattle and keeps the town in meat, but there is little of the town left; he runs a store, but there are few customers; he has a branch store at the Batavia goldfields nearly seventy miles to the northward, but the miners, with one or two exceptions, hardly earn cigarette papers. I do not think he makes very much of a living, depending, I gathered, on private means. I think he would stay at Coen, because of old associations and because the place is undeniably healthy and beautiful; but his two young daughters, at school in the South, are approaching the flapper stage, and he and his wife realize that it would not be kind to keep them in Coen. He, I suspect, will soon leave. Mr. Shepherd, the other storekeeper, with great cattle interests in the neighbourhood, will most probably remain to keep the police headquarters and the telegraph station alive.

There is something very sad in a dying town. While we were in Coen, it had been decided to close the school; the settlement can only offer eight children now, and ten are required. The schoolmaster, who had been in Coen for some years, was not happy about this; but I don't think it is really bad fortune to be dragged from a decaying town or settlement; many promising lives are wasted in them.

Still Coen appears a most cheerful place. Such houses as remain do not look decayed or tired ; the people have fine gardens, and the place was alight and gay with truly lovely crimson flamboyant trees, great splotches of purple bougainvillea, and many frangipani-trees.

But I have, although not designedly, left to the last what we thought was the best of Coen - Mrs. Armbruist. I have tried again and again to capture her with my pen (a typewriter as a matter of fact), but now abandoning sheets and sheets of paper, I offer a precis of what I have written:

About thirty-five, with brick-red hair-thinking often about the two daughters at school South - keeping their room pretty like a doll's house, all pale blue with cream curtains and snowy mosquito-nets - a marvellous housekeeper and a superb cook - and a great gardener - does not know she is clever - not humble, not belligerently modest, but most attractive when she does not realize what that clean sweet bedroom and that excellent cool meal with the tomato salads and green vegetables mean to tired travellers - gives the general impression in anxious glances that her guests are worth much more than she can do for them. So much for the precis!

How our car was packed when we left! I think Mrs. Armbruist believed we were travelling in a mighty pantechnicon as big as her heart. A rich cake measuring two feet by two feet, chock-a-block with fruit, and surely compounded of dozens of eggs, was stowed somewhere. Four dozen eggs were packed and hidden in dangerous places, Two quart bottles of creamy goat's milk were jammed behind my seat. The tucker-box was packed with a cold joint of roast kid, four loaves of fresh bread, pots of jam, bottles of hoarhound beer, and other offerings.

Mr. Armbruist lent us a native to guide us by a short cut to the telegraph-line. The line passes through Coen, but the country, still under the influence of the McIlwraith Range, is very rough for a mile or two out of the town and the native guide would lead us to a point where it became flat. The telegraph-line would now be our guide for the rest of the long journey, although as it turned out we left it between Mein and Moreton.

Only one car had ever got farther north than Coen, that of the Flying Missionary. Very soon, now, we shall reach the point where he, alas, met his Waterloo; and then our car becomes the pioneer car, the smallest and the greatest in Australia!

The Flying Missionary, the Reverend John Flynn, with a cantakerous vehicle.

10

Coen to Mien

I FEAR it will be something of an effort for me to retain my readers' interest on much of the remaining part of our journey. I suspect that our story may be digested most comfortably if taken with a map. Coen can be easily discovered; Mein will appear almost due north at the end of a thin line marking the telegraph. I propose now to tell of our adventures between these two places. "The terrible Archer" is what we dread most - the Archer River.

The telegraph-line passes right up the centre of the Peninsula and hops off near Cape York for Thursday Island. Telegraph communication with Thursday Island is the chief reason for the line's existence. But, apart from Thursday Island, of immense tactical importance in the event of war, the line actually keeps the Cape York Peninsula alive. We heard rumours, very sad rumours, that wireless would do away with the telegraph. But these, I dare say, are groundless; no government would allow economy to kill so vast an area of Australia. Frankly it is with something of a shudder that I recall these rumours, thinking of the few people living in the Peninsula and of what the closing down of the line would mean to them.

The telegraph-line - a single line on slim posts of iron (because of the white ants) - is tapped by a telegraph office about every seventy miles. Each office employs three persons, a telegraphist, a linesman, and a labourer. When the telegraphist is married, his wife takes the position of one of the other two - the labourer, I presume she would say. In that wild country three are vitally necessary; a man should never be alone.

Each station has one bungalow and a humpy or two. The bungalows are all of a pattern, and a very pleasant pattern indeed. Each house is built in the form of a square on a platform ten feet high. There is a wide veranda round the outside and a narrower one surrounding the well formed by the square. The well is generally unroofed, although at Cape York it has been floored and roofed, forming a cool living-room. At two diagonally opposite corners are projections of steel with loopholes, each commanding two sides of the bungalow. These were designed to repel native attack, but, now that the natives are very tame, the little projections come in handy for bathrooms and kitchenettes. Each bungalow has eight immense tanks - placed under the house and therefore safe from hostile interference. The tap of each tank can be locked; water is not plentiful at all stations, and rigid economy must be practised during the long dry season of sometimes nine months. The bungalows have eight rooms each and are made almost entirely with corrugated iron. The fact that their proportions are excellent and that they all seem to be kept freshly painted removes the usual ugly effect of corrugated iron.

The telegraph-line is kept cleared about twenty feet on each side ; but this simply means that once a year the underbrush is lopped off a foot or so from the ground. Fortunately most of the old tree trunks and stumps have been eaten by white ants since the line was projected; but a good many remain. The cut underbrush is something of a nuisance, since there remain sharp little stakes capable of piercing the best rubber. Ant-heaps appear everywhere, and they must be knocked down when possible. As a matter of fact some of the ant-heaps require dynamite to knock them down, for they reach as high as twenty-four feet. The white ants have been known to "earth" the line by building their castles right up to, and even through it within a week or two.

The line was our guide and a constant assurance of safety. We had tried to borrow a portable telephone so that we might tap in, but the official we saw, while regretting his inability to lend us one, whispered: "People in difficulties have been known to break the line - most annoying for the linesman, who must repair the break at once!" When I mentioned to the telegraphist at Coen that we would break his line in the event of serious difficulty, he said primly -"Do! I'll come out to you all right - but I'll be a little saucy!"

Two or three pads or bridle-tracks follow the line. Where the country suits it, the line goes straight across rivers and gulches, not being concerned with pedestrians, equestrians, and least of all, motor traffic. The pads are made by the linesmen, by the mailman, by cattle being driven north to Red Island, and by police patrols. It is therefore sometimes possible to keep two wheels of a car safe from punctures.

Almost the whole journey is made through forest. The view on each side is nearly always blocked by gum-trees. By the way, the fact that every telegraph-post bears a number allows one to know to a fraction of a mile the distance run. The posts begin with "I" at the telegraph station and go on rising to precisely half-way between stations; from half-way the numbers diminish, until the next station is reached. This is quite entertaining, and passes the time not spent in repairing punctures.

From Coen onwards we averaged six punctures a day; between McDonnell and Cape York we enjoyed some twenty-five. Just after Coen we lost the wheel-nut spanner, and the job of getting the wheels off with a shifting spanner through the fine spokes inspired some serious cussing.

We left Coen at about ten o'clock in the morning. For an hour or two the country, still affected by the McIlwraith Range, remained undulating, but the range gradually swept to our right, and we were on fairly flat country except when the land sunk to, or rose from, rivers and creeks. The going would have been good were it not for long patches of an abomination called grass-tree. The grass-tree is an exceedingly pretty shrub or palm, but we learned to detest the vista of fresh green which it offered along the clearing. It is a fat, fibrous, juicy kind of little black trunk ending in a fine burst of reed-like spears of rich green. It may grow to a height of six feet, but more generally averages about four feet. The very low grass-trees, say about two feet, are to the inexperienced most dangerous. They will bend most obligingly before the axle of a car, but once under, they seem to rise up and play the very devil with the various gadgets underneath, being quite capable of bending light steel rods and buckling running-boards. An innocent-looking grass-tree cracked our tucker-box; another almost ruined our chance of selling the Baby to that rich prospect on Thursday Island, by buckling and breaking a running-board.

From ten in the morning until about six in the evening we struggled through this grass-tree country, but in that time we had covered twenty miles, which we thought very good. We found a fine camp near some long, narrow, deep lagoons, an eerie kind of place said to be snake-infested. The more or less cleared space where linesmen camp showed many snake trails; and so we walked very warily. It was the coupling season for brown snakes in the Peninsula, but of this we were blissfully ignorant.

Although we were utterly tired that evening the heat and flies had been very trying-sleep could not be thought of. After an excellent dinner for which we thanked God and Mrs. Armbruist, I began repairing tyres, while Dick proceeded to make what seemed a neat little table napkin ring. Actually he was trying to replace what I presume might be called a gland washer, which had been dragged out by grass-tree. I am not mechanical, but I try to explain by saying that this ring, in two sections, fits round the main shaft as it enters that leather bellows-like bag which protects the universal joint under the car. I don't know what a universal joint is, but I easily saw that if this bag should fill with rubbish it might be disastrous.

The materials at Dick's disposal were not promising, nor were the tools - our wooden number-plate of inch timber, a sheath-knife, and an iron tent-peg. He managed to cut off a corner of the name-plate with his knife, no easy task; he bored a hole with the heated tent-peg, and carved the thing down to the appearance of a wooden napkin ring. Then he split it - with grave danger - and the job was done. It occupied some four hours. It sounds a small thing to rave about, but I always regard that little job as among the many bright efforts my friend carried off on this trip.

In the meantime, after the punctures had been sworn right, I plucked and cleaned a great scrub turkey which we had shot during the day. Again I stuffed the fat carcase with onions and mangoes (with pepper and salt thrown in) and the poor fat turkey spent its last night as a mere turkey getting sweetly tender for the morrow.

Now that sounds very cold-blooded; and yet -and it is excessively weak of me to admit it - I hate killing. Since the war, I have never killed anything for mere sport. Nor can I. Dick shot that turkey from the car, and, it being a moving and difficult target, he only wounded it. I ran to catch it. As I approached, I saw a look of deadly fear in the turkey's eyes, and I can still see that look. I love animals; I am one of those lucky beings who are trusted by birds and beasts. They usually give me the friendliest of glances, or at the worst a look of confident caution; that turkey did not. I have no idea why I offer this ; it is part of the day's impressions.

We were up at dawn the next morning and ready to start within a remarkably short time. We had but forty miles before us, and given freedom from grass-tree, we thought we might strike Mein that night. We were hurrying. The few people we had met were praying for rain ; there was now a very real danger that their prayers would be answered. We wanted to join in those prayers - at Cape York. Two or three thundershowers would end our expedition.

Alas, Deep Creek (aka Peach Creek), a few miles on from our camp, occupied most of our morning. We saw it first from the telegraph clearing - a great chasm fifty feet deep with precipitous sides. It meant reconnoitering along the banks for some distance in order to find the possible crossing suggested by Mr. Armbruist.

As usual, we got into the creek-bed all right; but, once in, it was some time before we could find a way out. Eventually we had to run down the creek some fifty yards - a horrible business, getting over odd rocks, tree-roots, and beds of soft sand - until we found ourselves near a cattle-pad climbing the far bank. We navvied for nearly four hours, and then, with block and tackle to help, we struggled to the far bank.

I note that Deep Creek has occupied but a paragraph; Dick and I feel that our recollections of Deep Creek should occupy ten volumes, not for children!

And now, at last, we were pioneer motorists.

No car under its own power had ever reached farther north. For here, at Deep Creek, the Flying Missionary ceased to fly in his rich American car.

He, like us, had got into Deep Creek all right; but he was too optimistic in his effort to run up the far bank. Actually, he reached to within a few feet of the top when his engine gave out. He was now in grave danger, for the grade is almost upright, and the track simply wide enough for a car, while on one side are great rocks falling in steps to the river-bed. The car began backing.

I am not very clear about what now happened. But it seems that some misguided soul had told the missionary to put his gears in low (forward) to help the brakes if he wanted to stop on a steep hill. That, of course, might help sometimes; but it seems to me the counsel of desperation on a very steep rise with all the weight of the car dragging back. Once more I must admit being unmechanical; but of course anyone can see that an engine engaged on very low forward speed would suffer seriously if the car backed.

I suspect that if he had put his gears in reverse, the brakes would have been helped and the mechanics of the car not seriously hurt. However, with great good luck, that wonder car backed down into the river-bed in safety - apparently. But only apparently. For when, after more work on the road, the missionary drove furiously and successfully to the top of Deep Creek bank, the clutch arrangements refused to clutch any more, and the car was dead. It is amazing to realize that the stripped gear wheels permitted so much. If they had not, it would have been farewell to the car. The floods would soon have swept it to the Gulf of Carpentaria.

Having plenty of provisions and glorious spirits (nothing ever worries the Flying Missionary or his wife), they sent their native servant back to Coen for help; and after a day or two a slightly depressed cavalcade (hurt in its pride more than anything else), consisting of a considerable "plant" of pack - and riding-horses, began the slow but secure journey to Weipa. Weipa may be seen on the map on the Embley River near Albatross Bay on the north-west coast of the Peninsula. The car remained at Deep Creek for some months. It was often in grave danger from bush-fires; but the linesmen kept the grass around it burnt, and in the fullness of time the missionary and his father-in-law led an expedition to salve it. They carried spare parts and a pair of mules, and what with the mules and many ropes, the car eventually reached Weipa. I hope to tell more of that wonder car when eventually. we reach Weipa.

In case it should be thought that I am laughing at our friend, I must hasten to point out that we had one great advantage - lightness. Another advantage was British workmanship. When it is remembered that we depended upon every item in our car standing up to the roughest kind of work - we carried no spares-it will be realized what a marvellous little engine we had. These foreign cars look much more exciting and rich than the British car; and of course many folks swear by them, and rightly perhaps; I can only offer our own experience.. Give me a British car any day in the week! Another point in our favour: the Flying Missionary was not an experienced driver at the time (which shows his great courage in attempting and nearly pulling off a mighty feat); Dick is. In fact I believe his perambulator, go-cart, or soap-box - whatever he used before he walked - had a motor in it. Still another point: Dick and I never took a chance when the slightest risk could be avoided. Cape York was before us when we left Sydney; it never left us until we reached it. We used to see Cape York when we were building roads out of creeks; and the roads were invariably made well. Fatigue never prevented Dick from getting under the car every night, and never prevented my cleaning and polishing the car - for the Thursday Island prospect!

Deep Creek has unfortunately a tributary a few hundred yards farther on which must be crossed. It is a shorter business, but not much sweeter. Then there were other creeks and watercourses, but luckily little grass-tree. We tried to reach "the terrible Archer" that day, but darkness and two punctures forced us to camp less than half a mile short of it.

When we saw it next morning, the sight was startling. In front of it the telegraph clearing fell in great ragged cliffs, reaching a mighty jumble of great round boulders, thirty and forty feet in diameter. The width of this jumble could hardly have been less than five hundred yards. The far bank, seen in the distance, appeared unpromising. The Archer was, of course, not running. Not long after we crossed it, it was running, and running furiously.

But as with all difficulties, a closer view of the Archer bed showed a way out. By following the pads, which now shook the dust of the clearing from their feet, we found a way into the river. We found a way to an island across soft sand. We went round the island and discovered a narrow track through the great boulders. We cut tracks through scrub, and after some hours of heavy work, we had marked a possible track. I shall never forget that morning. The river-bed became an oven, and at times we felt we could do no more. Nevertheless, by noon the car was up on the far bank, and the Archer beaten. We paused at a spot where Mr. Armbruist had been camping one night in apparent security, for the river was a long way below him. Within fifteen minutes he was sitting in the branches of a tree, while his plant (pack-horses, riding-horses, and provisions) was being swept to the sea. That, of course, was during the "wet"; but it will give some idea of what can happen in the Peninsula.

We had unpacked the car at the near bank, and when she was once more on the telegraph clearing with "the terrible Archer" behind her, I said, "Now - forget the baggage - let's swim in one of the deep pools among the rocks!"

"You can," said Dick courteously; "but I can't, with that damn baggage at the other side."

Therefore in sheer desperation we lugged load after load across the steaming oven. "Fools!" I often said to myself; "what are we doing this for?" Yet the last load reached the car, and almost gaily we ran down into the river-bed, making for the most commodious pool in the rock clefts.

We chose a pool near some shady trees; all these great rivers have trees growing in their beds, and although of the gum genus, they look remarkably like willows. Our pool, clear and moderately cool, had a minute island in its middle, and on this we placed all our soiled clothing, our shaving gear and soap, towels, tobacco, pipes and matches, and a large packet of raisins. We had, therefore, everything to make us happy. When bored with lolling in the pool, we washed clothes and put them out to dry on the hot rocks. We shaved and washed in another small pool near; we ate many raisins, separating them very carefully from the little white worms amongst them; and we smoked. A truly glorious three hours; I can recall none more so.

At three o'clock we were on our way once more, now determined to reach Mein that night. The going was extremely good, few creeks to hold us up and fairly flat land. But while we were seldom held up on this short section, we constantly ran the risk of being buried; for here we first met melon-holes.

Imagine a hollow melon with a diameter of anything from twelve inches to as many feet, sunk a few inches below the surface, with a small airhole hidden by tall grass. Imagine driving innocently over one; imagine the condition of a car, or of a horse for that matter, if the surface gives way, which of course it does, often. I have described the worst kind of melon-hole, but the worst are not uncommon. I cannot say how these curious caverns are formed. Apparently the earth's surface here becomes water-logged during the "wet," and this condition, followed by rapid baking in fierce sunlight, permits what were great bubbles to become - melon-holes. They are seriously dreaded by horsemen, and are often fatal to their animals. Melon-holes appear in patches, and at the first suspicion of melon-holes it is vitally necessary for one to walk ahead with a stick, trusting not one square yard of track. Occasionally we negotiated some hundreds of yards of melon-holes, only to find ourselves in a cul-de-sac from which we had to back in considerable danger.

However, long stretches of hard infertile country helped us considerably; once I saw the speedometer recording ten miles an hour during a few seconds-a record for the trip on cross-country work - and dusk found us, according to the telegraph-poles, three miles from Mein.

Prudence warned us to camp, with all these melon-holes about, but a desire to see other human beings in this wilderness urged us to push forward. It is better to depend entirely on the headlights in the bush than to trust to the uncertain light of dusk, and so we boiled the billy at a convenient place and began imagining the household *menage* at Mein. I saw the usual telegraph bungalow with a young telegraphist and a pleasant young wife. I saw a stretcher-bed made up on the veranda, and I even conceived what was waiting for us in the dining-room! I imagined palms and a fine garden around the bungalow. "You're very late, gentlemen," I said to Dick in a treble voice; "we gave you up when dusk fell ; we never dreamt you would come along the track in the dark. But comeand have some supper; we've killed a chicken for you."

"Oh thanks very much, Mrs. Mein," returned Dick; "you're very kind- where can I wash my hands? "

And so we yarned as we ate boiled eggs and chunks of Mrs. Armbruist's cake with tea. When it was dark, we defied the melons and pushed on. We could not now see the telegraph poles; we were on a pad a few yards within the forest, following the clearing, and so depended on the speedo¬meter register to find Mein. When the three miles were reduced to nothing we looked for lights, but saw none. Then we found the pad crossing the telegraph clearing. We noticed that some work had been done on a creek crossing, and, taking a very grave chance here, we crossed the creek and came to a halt in what seemed a veritable garden of melon-holes. We picked our way delicately, and eventually came to a bark humpy. We passed the humpy and paused.

Within thirty yards of us three men were sitting in the dark on the far side of a veranda, discussing no us, wondering whether Deep Creek or "the terrible Archer" had settled our mad enterprise. " They'll never do it! It can't be done in a car! " said one man. At that second they heard a triumphant blast from our motor-horn, and they came down to guide us.

There was no lady at Mein, but there were three fine men; and soon we were being treated with a kindness and delicacy not easy to express. There was Mr. Parker, the telegraphist, with a slight Irish accent; there were Mr. Thompson, the telegraph labourer, and Willie Bryant, the linesman, all living in the wildest spot on earth, I thought, and one of the ugliest and most cruel ; but the winner of the day's race in Sydney seemed to concern them all more than anything else ; and they struck me as being perfectly happy.

Mein and our short stay there require a new chapter.

11

Mein and Onwards

MEIN is well named. It is pronounced almost " mean," with slight accent on the "an."

Imagine a plain of baked melon-hole land with gum-trees rising from it. Imagine the telegraph bungalow without a green blade of grass within many miles. Imagine mighty tanks empty or with a few drops in one reserved for drinking. And, finally, imagine two middle-aged men and a younger man forced to live without adequate water for cleansing their home or their clothes. No green food, nothing but tinned tack (if possible), salt junk, and sometimes sweet potatoes. Day after day, week after week, month after month - even year after year. In a year, perhaps six fresh faces are seen. There is nothing to see but gum-trees and wallabies. The climate is intensely hot, and at Mein, breathless. During the "wet" the country is one vast and dangerous quagmire. And yet the business man on Thursday Island must be able to send his telegram through to Sydney (for which he pays one shilling). Faults in the line are therefore repaired at once, the linesman going forth in all weathers, risking his life hourly with devil-devil and melon-holes. Thirty-five miles on each side of the station must be patrolled, and that cannot be done in a day. The crossing of the creeks, which become great rushing rivers during the" wet," seemed to me extremely dangerous; but the linesmen make a boat with their tent tarpaulin and saplings, and ferry their gear across.

Life would seem almost impossible if it were not for horse-racing. The telegraph folks have their own reputable bookmakers in the cities, and nearly every day telegrams are exchanged. It seemed to me that what these men did not know about horses was not worth knowing; one or two of them actually make money. And yet few, if any, of them have even seen a racecourse.

"I suppose," said one man, "when you're in Sydney you go and have a *look* at 'em?"

He spoke almost reverently, as if to a Superior Being who had seen that which should not be seen.

In the evenings the telegraphists chat on the telephone with the other stations; and here at Mein we began making friends with the fellows farther north. They offered great encouragement and gave useful directions. They regretted that we had not allowed them more time to clear tracks for us.

We proposed to rest one day at Mein, chiefly to overhaul the car. It having been pushed under the house and into the cool inner court of the bungalow, Dick began his terrifying inspection.

It was most alarming because I constantly feared he might find something on the verge of collapse. Every now and then, while I polished the car's body, I would inquire anxiously, " Any interesting findings, Dick?" "No, not yet!" was all I could hope for.

The "interesting findings" remark is in our collection. A physician friend of ours used to send his X-ray cases to Doctor B., an X-ray specialist. Doctor B.'s job was simply to make photographs of the patients' "innards" and then to send them (the photographs) and the patients back to the physician. Having pocketed his five guineas, Doctor B. was supposed to resign all interest in the patients, who were either sent to a surgeon for surgical treatment or remained to be dieted into good health by the physician. But there came a day when Doctor B. wanted to improve his business; perhaps the poor man needed a new Rolls Royce ; at any rate, he composed a neat little form letter and sent it off to all the names on his book. "Dear Sir or Madame," it ran; "in view of the interesting findings shown in your X-ray photographs, I am wondering how you are keeping. Do not hesitate to call and see me, etc." The result was truly awful. Large numbers of the physician's patients besieged his surgery. "You told me I had nothing but a little weakness in my stomach; you have dieted me unpleasantly; you have told me that my X-ray showed a negative finding; and here this Doctor B. writes suggesting I have a GROWTH. And I always knew I had." Many of the patients wailed in this strain.

It was useless for our friend to point out that his patients had improved, even that some were cured. That "interesting findings" started them off again. Needless to say, Doctor B. was treated very tersely by the British Medical Association, and instead of finding additional interesting five guineas, he found himself short of five hundred guineas a year.

But Dick's inspection at Mein showed" negative findings; " the car was standing up well.

Willie Bryant remained near the car from eleven in the morning until four in the afternoon, with a short interval taken off for luncheon. I had said to him when Dick first started, "I'll get him to give you a ride, when he's finished."

Such a treat - Willie had never driven in a car before, and had not seen more than about three in his life could not be missed. Willie, as I heard him say to a friend, was not taking any chances of being forgotten.

When later in the afternoon he went for a short spin, he came back highly excited and greatly thrilled with the speed the little car had attained. "I thought," he said, "every tree would spell our end; the trees whizzed by!" Dick told me that he was greatly interested in seeing Willie pull in his head whenever he passed close to a tree. The great speed, by the way, was ten miles an hour, possible out of Mein because there is a blazed trail wide enough for a car. Willie wanted to buy our car, and offered a big sum in cash.

The Batavia gold-diggings are not far from Mein. We had hoped to take a run out to them, but we dared not spend the time. However, one of the miners or prospectors came in to the telegraph station during the day, and we had a yarn with him. He appears at Mein perhaps once in every four months; he considered himself very lucky to have struck the day of all days in the year when the first car should appear. By an unfortunate mischance the poor man had forgotten his false teeth - both top and bottom sets; but this gave him a gentle, motherly expression that was all to the good. "I always wear teeth," he explained, "when I come in to Mein; this is the first time I haven't-and here are visitors!"

This man carried with him seventy-five ounces of gold, four months' work. He showed us a few small nuggets which made us feel like abandoning all and taking to gold-mining; but, as he pointed out, he is lucky. His claim is the only one paying seriously at Batavia. Most of the other prospectors fail even to make "tucker."

During the afternoon another visitor turned up, Alick Thompson, a son of Mr. Thompson of Mein who is the mailman between Coen and Moreton via Merluna cattle-station and Weipa. This boy, with a plant of a dozen horses, has sometimes a very hard row to hoe. Mr. Parker very carefully packed up the miner's gold into small canvas bags. Alick took it south with him the following morning. What a chance for a bushranger!

It was curious to find so great a crowd concentrating at Mein that day. So many people had hardly ever been there together before.

Our route now lay to the west of the telegraph-line, Via Merluna to Moreton. Merluna, a vast state-owned cattle-station connected with Mein by telephone, had ten gallons of petrol ready for us. Alick seemed to think we could manage the trail from Merluna on to Moreton, and so we decided not to return to Mein. We also received a message from the Flying Missionary at Weipa begging us to call on him. He sent word that he had twenty cases of petrol, and that we could have the lot if we needed it. When we learnt that a wagon road connected Merluna with Weipa we did not hesitate. It was Saturday morning and we thought we might reach Weipa that evening - which sounds optimistic in view of the fact that the distance is seventy miles.

The road - hardly more than blazed trees between Mein and Merluna is something of a terror. Melon-holes are very plentiful. We nearly dived into the great melon which broke the Flying Missionary's axle some time earlier. Dick and I saw it together. Dick whizzed round the wheel, but I saw that he had chosen the less of two evils, for a great stump was immediately in front of our new course. But the brakes behaved well; the bonnet simply kissed the stump; and we were saved.

The Flying Missionary had no personal intention of diving into that melon-hole. He saw it, and was steering away from it when the passenger beside him on the front seat said gaily, "Give me the wheel - let me drive!"

When the missionary told us that story, he lifted his elbow suggestively and whispered, "Whisky!" And we understood.

We reached Merluna at about one o'clock.

The station seems rather like a village of small bungalows. There are many beautiful mango trees in the homestead clearing, and we caught a glimpse of a banana plantation. The station manager has a good many small children; the aboriginal servants have more; and the effect when we arrived was of a cheerful school during playtime. We were soon led into a large dining room, and here was spread a fine dinner. The station book-keeper is a brother of Willie Bryant of Mein. Like Willie, he is a good-looking young fellow, but alas, a serious fall from a horse, caused, if I remember rightly, by melon-holes, has seriously affected his health, and it is feared he will never ride again. The manager offered us twenty gallons of petrol, but we had now decided to buy what we needed from the Flying Missionary at Weipa.

While Merluna seemed cheerful and beautiful that day, it has a very sickly reputation. There is no decent spring or creek within many miles, and the homestead depends for household water on a great yellow, muddy pool. When we were there, one small tank was all the respectable water left on the place, and this was reserved for drinking, the tap being kept locked. Fever is the curse of Merluna, but I was unable to find out what kind, whether ordinary malaria or something else. Typhus germs would have a prosperous time here.

The station stretches from coast to coast of the Peninsula, and has an immense area. It does not pay. In fact we heard that it costs the Queensland Government some thousands a year to keep up. The manager told us that within six months it would be abandoned. He had then a large number of thoroughbred stock-horses on hand, and the best of these could be bought for a few pounds. The manager had ridden down from Cape York some time before; he told us that between McDonnell and Cape York the creeks had bridges across them wide enough for the car. He thought the Jardine River would prove difficult. It was very wide and always carried deep water. There were many crocodiles in it, and - what seemed very discouraging - no soft timber grew within some miles of the river-banks. The building of a raft would thus be a great difficulty.

We left Merluna after dinner and began the journey of forty-odd miles to Weipa. There is a good bush road, used by the Merluna people to carry stores from Weipa in a wagon; therefore we foresaw no trouble in reaching the Flying Missionary before dusk. But a bush road suitable for a large-wheeled wagon is often a trial to a motor. Often the tracks cut by the wagon-wheels were fifteen inches deep, and it was something of a job to keep the car from slipping in.

The Merluna manager had warned us that his wagon with a team of about thirty quadrupeds (I say that designedly!) would be met on the road; and he begged us to go warily. His beasts had never seen a car.

Sure enough, about a third of the way, we heard wild shouts. We immediately left the road, and entered the forest, making a wide half-circle around the strangest cavalcade I have ever seen. There were four donkeys, about six mules, and twenty horses, all harnessed together, drawing the great wagon. The horses were obviously very much alarmed, but remained tremblingly steady. The mules took little notice of us; but the donkeys were very bad indeed, bucking and jumping and evidently determined to upset the nerves of the team. Three or four blacks were driving, bullock-wagon fashion, but, while they wanted to come and see us, they dared not leave the team. We hurried away from them, not wanting to have a wrecked wagon on our conscience.

I may say here that in this baked country Dick and I were always very careful about fires, matches, and cigarette ends. Apart from the fact that carelessness might have meant our own cremation - for the grass is thick and sometimes four feet high - we naturally thought of the destruction which would follow a bush-fire.

We had not been driving very long after passing the wagon before we saw clouds of smoke coming towards us. Soon we were within a few hundred yards of a bush-fire which had obviously not been burning for long. Fortunately there was little or no breeze, and the fire was travelling slowly. Had we arrived half an hour sooner we could have saved Merluna from serious loss. I said to Dick, "We are going to be blamed for that fire!" It was obvious that the wagon-drivers were the culprits.

The great thing now was to decide what to do. Prudence suggested a return to Merluna, for the fire was advancing on each side of the road, but we wanted to see the Flying Missionary that night, and so we took the car back some distance and reconnoitered. Finally we set a match to the grass on each side of the road fifty yards ahead of the main fire, and thus cleared a space for the dash we proposed to make. Then by beating out the burning grass on the ridge between the wheel tracks on the road, we eventually saw our way through. The dash was a little dangerous, but wholly successful; we were soon through the fire, whose beginnings at the wagon-drivers' camp were quite clear. I noticed that hundreds of hawks were flying almost in the smoke, picking up semi-roasted dainties in the way of iguanas and small snakes.

The delay made us a trifle late in reaching Weipa. We saw and enjoyed again the same lovely effects of a sunset through tall trees, very similar to what we had seen on the night when we were approaching the Eighteen Mile. Although we were now near the Gulf coast, we were still in the forest, and inky darkness found us struggling within a mile or two of Weipa.

But blackest night could not kill the effulgent light which brightened that mission compound when the Flying Missionary discovered us!

There was a wild whoop of joy as a figure in white came dancing towards us. From dormitories and outbuildings poured forth dozens of native men, women, and children. The missionary was soon hoarse with excitement and joy. Yet I detected a slight note of melancholy, wholly boyish, when he said, "Ah - you have succeeded where I failed!"

"Not at all!" we encouraged playfully." You see," he said, "my car- !"

He went on to explain his difficulties during the journey north, but he had no blame for his car. How he loved it! If the excitement of the reception had not been so great, he would have led us instantly to his garage to admire it.

"Men and women-boys and girls!" he shouted to the glowing eyes around us; "come on, now-three cheers! Three cheers for these men!"

No second invitation was required. We all went mad, and the dark world around became a seething pool of wild excitement. Finally the missionary made a short effective speech, placing poor Dick and me in a most untenable position in the future children's history books of Australia!

When the excitement cooled a little, we were taken to the mission bungalow, and met the missionary's wife and small daughter. Our clothing was now in a shocking state, but fresh shirts were supplied, and after a good bath we were sitting round a table eating all kinds of pleasant food.

A dance was instantly arranged for the aborigines on the station. The missionary, still in a great state of enthusiasm, became very busy issuing sacks of flour, many pounds of sugar, and much tobacco. Eventually the beating of drums warned us to repair to the native village, and we saw the usual native dancing, robbed, in this case, of any interesting wickedness. Finally the missionary made a speech in polished English (so that we might understand) and I made one in "pidgin" which no one understood; but our goodwill was accepted - and so to bed!

A great chap, the Flying Missionary in the flesh! He is chock-a-block with enthusiasm, and he would need to be overflowing with it at Weipa. I have always noticed that mission stations are built on the most unsavoury and unhealthy spots available, where the missionaries can die of malaria and dysentery; but it seemed amazing to me to discover a Presbyterian mission placed in so abominable a hole. Within two miles of Weipa is a pleasant valley of rich black soil with a permanently running creek; within ten miles are dozens of excellent spots with fresh water; but Weipa depends on tanks and a great foul muddy pool. The mission tries to teach the aborigines agriculture, but the land around Weipa is baked hard during eight months of the year. It seems against the nature of Scots caution.

Yet the mission performs a great work. Our host had started a timber industry, and a Fordson tractor was doing good work for him. He was trying to inculcate the idea of village life, and, as far as I could see, he was enjoying a spot of success. But the best influence, surely, was on the children. We saw scores of little black girls and boys living in spotless dormitories, the girls learning to sew, to cook, and even to crochet, while the boys were taught gardening and other trades. The mission has certain judicial powers, and natives from afar can be committed to it and placed under the complete power of the missionary. He told us he had even a small prison.

We went to church the following morning and again in the evening. We were the only shabby persons present. The native children and women were exceedingly clean and starched; even the men wore collars and ties; and altogether kirk at Weipa followed the good Presbyterian fashion of being clean before the Lord. There was a fine smell of scented soap.

The missionary preached a sermon more than half an hour long at the morning service, and one slightly longer in the evening. Although the service was far from short, no native eye ever left the missionary's face from the moment he opened with prayer until he closed with a benediction.

I enjoyed both sermons, but the evening one better. The text - "Almost thou persuadest me to be a Christian" - from the Acts of the Apostles, gave the missionary fine scope for his descriptive powers, his great eloquence, and I think his sense of the ridiculous. The beautiful little mission chapel was steamingly hot, so that it will not seem strange if I confess to a longing for an iced drink. Unattainable iced beer at that moment seemed more attractive than a casket of diamonds. In the meantime the preacher was reaching his climax. I was perhaps sorry to think of his ending, but seriously looking forward to a drink of coolish water.

"Almost thou persuadest me to be a Christian," the missionary shouted, and every dark-brown eye was fixed on him. "Almost - almost - almost!

"But no - King Herod did not decide. He rose up with his "fancy woman" - that Bernice, and went to the palace gardens, where there were cool fountains and laughing flowers - cool fountains besprinkling the cool scent-laden air. His fancy woman - Bernice - he chose! And what was it - despite all the dignity of rustling silks, cool fountains, and flowers? What was it, my friends? "

With all this talk of cool fountains and cool scent-laden air, my thirst became almost un¬bearable. I swallowed a little and became thirstier.

"What was it?" again the missionary shouted. "It was," he answered - "nothing but a bottle of beer at a picnic!"

That finished me; but thank goodness a hymn was announced. I took courage when I saw that my hostess was barely suppressing merriment, or I imagined she was. To make quite sure, I mentioned that bottle of beer at luncheon, and both host and hostess laughed.

The missionary and his wife are always cheerfully laughing at themselves; they have not the slightest objection to adding to the joy of nations by telling stories against themselves. They took turns in offering their experiences with the wonder car.

Of course we saw and admired the car. We listened to the engine purring, and said, "Wonderful - very sweet, like new!" The missionary smiled. "What do you use to keep her paint so brilliant - and the leather work?" we murmured. "The car looks as if she's just come out of a show-roo!" The missionary beamed.

We were exaggerating a little; but the car appeared in very good condition and the engine certainly ran sweetly. And there is every reason in the world why that car should rattle like an antique sewing-machine. Roads on that flat country are easily made, and labour is not scarce. Therefore the missionary can often go for long spins on his home-made roads. Of course he cannot get away from his district to civilized roads with any degree of safety.

Once he attempted to motor to the mission station seventy miles to the north of him. He reached the place with great success, but when crossing a sandy flat on the return journey, the tide caught him, and his car was left overnight in the raging waves. When the tide went out, the natives rescued the car, and the missionary drove it home. Once home, it refused to go any more, and spare parts had to be sent for. Our hostess thought this little experience most amusing!

But I like best the story of the motor spin to York Downs. York Downs, a deserted cattle-station about sixteen miles along the road from Weipa to Merluna, can offer many excellent mangoes and other tropical fruits. The missionary's car contained his wife, his small daughter, his mother-in-law and his father-in-law, together with a few odd natives. They sped gaily to York Downs without noticing a stump in the middle of the road, leaning slightly, and leaning away from Weipa. The car may have given a slight bump when it passed over the stump, but there was no obvious effect on that rough road. The road was built for a high wagon, and many stumps remain along its middle.

They were returning with a good load of fruit, and very happy after the day's outing. Alas, that leaning stump rose a trifle at the first impact of the car going at about fifteen miles an hour, for it was now leaning towards the approaching car. It stood upright! The car stopped with a ghastly jolt and rose almost upright on its front wheels. The missionary was impaled on the steering-wheel; his wife and daughter shot over the windscreen on to the bonnet (fortunately the hood was down), and the in-laws shot from the back seat to the front. Luckily no one was seriously hurt.

The stump buckled the steering-rods and bent the axle so that the front wheels were turned towards each other; and the differentials were almost torn out. And yet the missionary drove that car home. The engine went all right, and he discovered that two natives, running alongside the car with long stakes which they used as levers, could keep it pointing in the right direction.

Our hostess told us that story with great esprit. The missionary sold us all the petrol we could carry, and we left Weipa soon after lunch the next day.

Two mission boys, Norman and George, had left Weipa early that morning. Their job was to walk the twenty odd miles to Cox's Creek, some six miles onward towards Moreton telegraph station from York Downs, at which point we proposed to leave the road for the cross-country trek now before us. We expected to find them at Cox's Creek that night ready to prepare the crossing.

The missionary accompanied us four miles along the road and then left us with his blessing.

We motored swiftly along the bush road and reached York Downs at about five o'clock. Here we found a number of native stockmen from Merluna busily burning the grass around the deserted homestead. Near the gates we saw the manager. Evidently the bush-fire had become serious.

"Now for it, Dick!" I whispered; "he's going to give us blazes for that fire; he's certain to have blamed us."

We therefore approached very delicately with charming smiles.

"We didn't do it - I know you believe we did," I said quickly.

The manager laughed, and then became very serious as he said: "That fire is still raging; it's destroyed thousands of acres of grass country; and only by working night and day, releasing horses and cattle from paddocks, have we saved what could be saved ! "

"But we didn't start it ! " I insisted.

"No, you didn't!" admitted the manager judicially, with a faint note of disappointment in his tones.

I saw at once that we had been blamed and possibly cursed; I wondered how our innocence had been established, for the evidence must have seemed strong against us.

"Yes, I blamed you," continued the manager.

"'City fellows all over - no consideration for the man on the land - dropped cigarette ends - fires not put out!' I said to myself. But coming along here this morning I saw your car tracks over freshly scorched grass. I knew then that you could not motor over country you had burnt yourselves, that the fire had begun before you arrived."

"Well," said Dick, "we're glad to hear that; we're not the kind of people to set fire to any man's land!" Which shoved the manager over to the defensive.

"Mission boys!" said he contemptuously; "and if I report the matter to the Weipa missionary I shall be told that my own boys did it." The manager laughed sarcastically.

"Which in this case," I said, up in arms for the missionary, "would be perfectly correct. That fire started in your wagon-drivers' camp." And I explained what we had seen.

It has since occurred to me that without our car tracks on that scorched grass, the evidence against us would have been stronger than that against the wagon-drivers; perhaps they, too, were innocent!

The fire, incidentally, raged for some weeks, burning many thousands of acres of grass.

12

To Moreton Telegraph Station and Onwards

WE have nearly two hundred miles yet to cover; but now that we have reached a point where no other motor-car has ever been seen, I am forced to the conclusion that what proved most difficult and trying to us, cannot be made interesting any longer. I have described the country-gum-trees in a continuous forest, cleft by that long clearing of the telegraph, great dry rivers, creeks, and watercourses. I have told of our daily work - navvying.

Therefore I have decided to ask my readers to take much of the remainder of our trek as read like the minutes of a dull meeting. I will hurry on, merely telling of particular adventures and of the few men and women we met on the way. But the scores of miles of silence must be imagined long intervals where we saw no other living soul. Then our condition must be conceived - and our appearance! We were growing very weary, living, I think, on a reserve of strength, buoyed up with a passionate desire, not unmindful of that rich prospect on Thursday Island, to get through to Cape York. We were a trifle nervous. We knew that an accident twenty miles short of Cape York would mean the waste of all our effort; and the car would not be ours! We were in rags, and hardly respectable; but the climate is warm, and a condition of nudity, while shocking to the blacks, would not have hurt us. They were glorious days. Every day was a glorious day, making up a parcel of the best days I have ever lived. Dick was very eager to reach Cape York, and so was I; but I felt a little sad at the thought that, in connecting once more with civilization at Thursday Island, the Great Adventure would end.

Norman and George, the mission boys lent by the Flying Missionary, had not got very far past York Downs. Apparently the temptation to gossip with the native fire-fighters had been too great; and we found them little more than two miles along the pad which leaves the road at York Downs for Moreton. We had hoped they would reach Cox's Creek that night, and be ready for the crossing of it at dawn, for we wanted to cover the forty miles to Moreton in one day. However, they seemed very tired; it was getting late; and so we camped.

The next morning I conceived the notion of walking with George, while Dick took Norman, a great hulking stout native, on to Cox's Creek.

At Cox's Creek, Norman did a certain amount of work, but not much. When George and I reached the car there was still much to be done. However, the additional weight of these two boys helped considerably, and Cox's was soon behind the car. The next bad creek, Moonlight, was said to be six miles farther on. But when again I walked with George it turned out to be nearer eight, and seemed a hundred. When I reached Moonlight, a great chasm of a ditch, I was in a very bad humour and be-haloed with a spirit of heroism. When Moonlight was finished with, I said a little peevishly to Dick:

"No - I don't think I can walk any more today - twelve miles in this heat, punctuated with navvying, has been enough, thanks!"

"Well," said he with a sour expression on his usually cheerful face," I'd rather have you beside me - or a bunch of lavender, than Norman!" Which told a story!

However, it is said that we whites offer an effluvium to dark persons hardly more attractive.

There were four bad crossings on this section of our journey - Cox's Creek, Moonlight Creek, Necktie Creek, and Lydia Creek; moreover there was at times a sad combination of melon-holes and devil-devil. Nothing approaching a road appeared; it was now a case of merely following pads through a forest with occasional open spaces. Lydia was easily the worst, and here again we narrowly missed disaster. I will try to explain what happened.

The boys had been left some miles behind, for occasionally we could make little spurts and we always went faster than a walking pace. We decided to get down the very steep near bank of Lydia, and by that time we thought the boys would catch up to us to help with the get-out.

Lydia is fifty feet deep, and her near bank falls almost sheer. The pad, a narrow track, cuts diagonally across the bank and descends in a very steep grade. On one side is the steep bank; on the other a precipitous drop to the rocky river-bed. We discovered that with a little work this pad could be induced to take the car wheels; but since our brakes were now in very bad condition, we decided to attach block and tackle to the rear axle and a tree, and gradually to let the car move slowly down. Unfortunately, the only tree near the top was about a yard down the bank ; but we knew that the car would not get up dangerous speed before the strain would be taken by the rope which was lying between the rear wheels and the front. It will be understood that when the car moved, the rear wheels should have passed over the ropes with the block and tackle. They would take the strain, and I should be ready to slacken the end rope, which I held near the bottom of the track.

Dick got into the car and began to drive.

Slowly the rear wheels passed over the tackle, but to my horror, I saw that the ropes had become entangled with the wheels, thus rendering the tackle useless. If I pulled now, I might affect the delicate steering of the car; and if the car refused to respond to brake pressure, it would be dragged back by the fouled rope - and the precipice was within a few inches of her wheels!

I yelled to Dick to stop. He jammed on the brakes, but the car continued to move. I had now reached the bonnet; and by exerting all my strength, I found I could stop her. If I had only thought to pick up a rock at the bottom for a chock; but I had not. There I was, shoving with all my power and searching hopelessly for a chock. There was none; and 1 dared not leave the car to find one. Moreover I knew that I could not continue to hold her indefinitely; in fact my strength was giving out.

"Get out!" I ordered Dick, but he said nothing. I could see his anxious face, and I continued: "Your life," I whispered, "is more valuable than any damn car - get out! "

"I will not I " he said.

I glanced at the rocky ravine fifty feet below us. Within a few minutes, I knew, the car would be down there, smashed to atoms.

"Please, please get out, old chap!" I begged.

"Wait a minute - just a minute! Can you hang on a second or two longer?" he asked calmly. "She'll be apples!" (Dick's jargon for "all right")

I nodded, and exerted all my strength; but the car was pushing me. My feet - 1 could see all my toes through the worn canvas shoes - were grinding and slipping against the baked earth. The situation was becoming hopeless.

In the meantime, with one hand dragging at the brake lever, and one foot pressed on the brake pedal, Dick stretched his spare hand over the door. Very carefully he opened the tucker-box. From this he subtracted a tea-billy. The billy had been jammed into a rough wedge some weeks earlier by grass-tree and, although straightened out again still remained something of a wedge.

At any rate, but little pressure would restore the wedge.

Dick handed this over the windscreen to me.

I jammed it under the front wheel nearest the precipice - and we were saved ! Curiously, when I lifted my head from the ground, I saw Norman and George standing above me. They had that moment arrived.

After Lydia the going was not very bad. Within a few miles of Moreton we met Mr. Burton, the linesman, who, with a canvas water-bottle slung over his shoulder, had come out to meet us.

At about six o'clock we were within a few hundred yards of the telegraph station bungalow; but between it and us ran the great Batavia River. The Batavia is never dry; but at this time the water was a series of long deep pools connected by shallow water running swiftly over what was something closely akin to quicksand. The river has great sandy banks nearly a hundred feet high, and the process of getting across promised to be very difficult, until the honking of our horn produced three men from the bungalow. They showed us a good way down to the river-bed, and their strength kept the poor little car's engine just moving when, with great difficulty, we pushed our way up the sandy bed of shallow running water to the track out of the river. We had to cross a narrow channel of fairly deep water, but a sack over the radiator kept the water out when Dick made a rush at it. He was rather proud of this rush, and impressed the telegraph men considerably when he kept going and reached the top of the far bank with a great flourish.

Curiously, within a week of our passage of the Batavia, the river became a rushing torrent. Tributaries draining thousands of square miles had been filled by thunderstorms and cloudbursts.

Another Bryant brother, Joe, was the acting telegraphist at Moreton. Mr. Burton, whom we had met a few miles along the pad, is the linesman and apparently the mess secretary. The labourer, Mr. Cottrel, was enjoying his annual holiday like a busman - on the spot. He has a fine little humpy of his own and a good garden; he is no longer young, and Moreton, though isolated, is a charming spot.

Here there is always plenty of water; an aboriginal camp within a few hundred yards of the station offers adequate labour for gardening and watering; and generally Moreton has a cheery, happy air, not so apparent at the other stations.

That first night we were much too fatigued to do more than sleep and eat, but the next day, which we decided to take off as a holiday, was spent largely in the Batavia with the telegraph men. There are crocodiles, but the pools near the station are generally free of them during the dry. In the wet season they are plentiful, and care must be taken.

A great place, Moreton, with its beautiful mango-trees, oranges, lemons, and bananas ; but I was most interested in the aboriginal camp.

I think I can give a slight impression of the blacks by describing what happened in the camp when the very tired Norman and George eventually reached it that night. They had immediately come to us for rations, and, when we had satisfied them, they repaired to the camp to share what they had. After the reception ceremonial they had as big a feast as possible and sat around the fire to gossip. Like all dark races, the blacks are highly emotional; sorrow and wailing may succeed joy and laughter within a few seconds. Therefore imagine Norman and George sitting near that fire with their hosts and a few hostesses in the offing, for women are duly humble in black society. Near the social circle is a small heap of roasted yams and sweet potatoes, also odd chunks of damper. The gentlemen smoke, eat, and talk; the ladies listen and discuss the news in whispers.

"Bili Baki got stabbed by a Malay on Thursday Island," said George conversationally.

"Have some more sweet potato! " invited a host, holding one out across the fire.

"Bili Baki stabbed by a Malay " whispered a gin to another gin. "When this happen? " she inquired of her husband in a humble whisper.

"Oh, two year ago, now," said Norman, munching his sweet potato.

"Who this feller-Bili Baki?" further inquired the gin.

"Mother-belong-him is Mini Eat-wallaby-quick, who live at Weipa in the Mission."

"Then," groaned the gin, " his father is Joni Emu-feet, whose mother was Tiri Mumu, whose uncle was Kaka Tiki who belong this nation. Aue-aue-ogord-boo-yaa-ooo!"

Within ten seconds, divested of all their clothing, every gin in the camp was dancing around the camp-fire emitting the most soul-stirring yowling I have ever heard. Never was such a sound. Five million cats making love at midnight could not have surpassed the Moreton gins. And yet the men continued detached, smoking, eating, and talking. The noise could be heard miles away. "A corroboree," explained the telegraph men.

"We simply must go and see it!" I said.

"They'll stop when they see us," said Mr. Burton.

Nevertheless we stole noiselessly along the pad to the camp, and saw much until the camp dogs smelt us and gave an alarm which sent the women scurrying into their bark huts.

I tried very hard to get the gins started again; but they could not yowl to order. In fact Bili Baki was forgotten two minutes after our arrival.

Of course it was quite within the bounds of probability that Bili Baki was not stabbed by a Malay, that he was alive and well. If Bili is still alive, the gins of Moreton will hear of it in 1939, and will instantly arrange a dance of rejoicing. They will not be annoyed with Norman or George. A travelling black without news of a startling character is a poor sort of visitor!

Before leaving Moreton we had a chat on the telephone with Mr. Hayes, the telegraphist at McDonnell, the last station before Cape York. He seemed seriously distressed about us. The blacks, he said, were encamped near the water-holes, where they could kill all the game they needed; they were therefore not eager to work. Tobacco might tempt them. He believed we could not progress from the Dulhunty River to the Jardine without native help. Speed, he believed, was now important. The weather might break at any time. He further explained that his linesman was then encamped at the Dulhunty, twenty odd miles south of McDonnell. The linesman was trying to get blacks for us. He urged us to hurry through; he hoped very sincerely that we should reach him.

"Turkey-brush," he said, "will be your greatest trouble."

Constable Pitchem had not mentioned turkey-brush; we wondered if it meant devil-devil, melon-holes, grass-tree, ridges.

We left Moreton as early as possible the next morning, with some hope of reaching the Dulhunty that night; but a creek called Spear and a river called Ducie held us up four hours, and we were forced to camp fifteen miles south of the Dulhunty. Otherwise the country was not difficult, and we covered the fifteen miles the following morning.

We found Mr. Fussle's camp near the telegraph clearing on the banks of the Dulhunty-a charming river which always runs well, with eight feet of sparkling water in it sweeping over pink and white sandstone and keeping alive true tropical vegetation along its banks. And a very kind Dulhunty, for at intervals it spreads over platforms of smooth stone, becoming quite shallow and making a comfortable ford.

Mr. Fussle, the McDonnell linesman, a good-looking young fellow, stepped from his tent to greet us.

"Well," said he, after the usual greetings, "you've got this far; I don't think you'll get much farther."

"Why not? " I asked.

Mr. Fussle went through a list of terrors which sent my spirits down to zero. "It had the curious and absurd effect of making me fix the blame for their existence on Mr. Fussle. I detest hearing of anything unpleasant ahead of me, and when the gentleman had been going through his list for some minutes, I made a valiant effort to switch his mind to happier channels. It might be interesting to observe how far my effort succeeded.

"Been camped here long, Mr. Fussle?" I asked pleasantly.

"Two months, now-no feed for the station horses at McDonnell; I watch them down here. Then there's Porcupine Creek-a stinger; you'll never get across Porcupine -"

"D'you ever go south?"

"Expect to in three months' time-then Buckboard Creek - no idea how you'll manage it - bridges, yes, but they only cross the permanent channel of the great creeks, down at the bottom - you've got to get down to the bridge - and up from it -"

"Your wife's here, isn't she?"

"In the tent - then Cholmondely Creek - a corker - great slabs of hard sandstone - then turkey-brush - oh, it's out of the question. Then, I forgot, there's--"

"Oh-forget them-forget them!" I urged, I fear a little impatiently; "let's rest for an hour or two!"

Mrs. Fussle now appeared, and the atmosphere, merely cloudy

through my stupid impatience and ostrich-like view of life, instantly cleared.

Mrs. Fussle is quite young. Until three years ago she lived in an important Victorian town; during the last three years she came to McDonnell as a bride - she has not seen another white woman. Much of her time is spent at the station bungalow, where her superb housekeeping makes life splendid for the men; but during four or five months of the year she camps with her husband at the Dulhunty, where there is enough grass to keep the telegraph-station horses alive. Fortunately, she adores Mr. Fussle!

I have no idea how Mrs. Fussle managed to produce so wonderful a luncheon; but there, in perhaps one of the wildest spots of Australia, we ate a delicious turkey curry with rice and mango chutney; followed a jelly, cooled in the Dulhunty, of soft apricots and sago.

After luncheon, Mr. Fussle, Dick, and I sat in the Dulhunty until our skin went crinkly. The water is very soft, and the washing of our frayed clothing was very easy.

The great question was now how to rope in blacks. Mr. Fussle offered little hope and seemed to think we should wait a day or two until some of them wandered to his camp. But we dared not wait. Provisions were getting scarce, and Mr. Hayes had told us that his store of flour was almost depleted. Flour would be necessary for the blacks we proposed to engage. At the moment when we had decided to walk to the Alice River native camp, a black appeared. Pointing at the sky (his clock) this black said he would return. with four others when the sun reached the horizon, He actually returned at eight o'clock and added himself and three others to our expedition.

We had our evening meal around the camp-fire. Another native, who appeared during the late afternoon, speared some interesting-looking fish, including black bream, and Mrs. Fussle made scones in her camp-oven. That little feast is chiefly associated in my mind with a remark made by Mrs. Fussle which became positively monotonous, yet very necessary -"Mr. Matthews - another scone?"

And that was not all. Before our bath in the Dulhunty, I had approached the tent with a cup to get hot water for shaving. "Ha!" said Mr. Fussle, "you've got your pannikin - let's put something in it!"

He put whisky in it - good Scotch; and he put some in Dick's cup

The car bogged near the Dulhunty River.

Tall white-ant hills just south of the McDonnell Telegraph Station.

and some in his own. It was all the liquor he had, and he had kept it for nine months.

Except for an occasional pull at a small bottle of Worcester sauce, that whisky was the only stimulant we tasted from Cooktown to the end of our journey. Whisky is more stimulating than sauce; but the sauce was not so bad.

We began the journey to McDonnell betimes in the morning. When staying with folks, we could never get away at dawn without being rude ; but the hours after dawn are the lovely hours in the tropics, and the only possible time to work. Our boys, Charlie, Peter, Mickie, and Joe, were great fellows. Charlie had a beard and one slightly white eye; Peter was the sheik of the party, being young and not ill-looking ; Mickie had been a native policeman and wore a small moustache; Joe had no distinguishing features. Mickie was the humorist of the party, as well as being something of a bush lawyer. Mickie would respond to the veriest shade of humour - the fun in small things and small remarks. As we progressed that day, I developed a habit of getting my names mixed. We were making for McDonnell; Moreton, of course, was behind us. But the fact that our progress was often very slow, especially at the creeks which were well up to Mr. Fussle's estimate, produced to Mickie, and indeed to me, some humour, when I would say, "Well, I hope we'll get to Moreton tonight! " I meant, of course, McDonnell; but Mickie saw the fun in the thought that our speed was so slow that it almost produced a retreat. And whenever I was about to get it right, saying, "Well, I think we'll get to -" Mickie would always add with a very grave look followed by a delicious laugh - " to Moreton!" I have laboured this point to show what I thought was a distinct sense of humour in the blacks, rather than a sense of fun common to dark people. That, of course, is only one incident; the whole journey was spent in laughing while these fine lads were with us.

They were true bush blacks, untouched by missions or serious white civilization, although Mickie had been a policeman. And their enthusiasm kept up from the moment we left the Dulhunty until very sadly we bade them good-bye at the Jardine. They were friendly, but always . respectful, and their devotion to us was very touching. Between creeks, we averaged a good six miles an hour ; but we had never to wait long for them. They always came running.

We crossed many creeks during that day, and these were now all running. The water was clear and beautiful; for the first time we travelled without carrying large quantities of water. Once the car got bogged; but this was so unusual an experience that we thought little of it.

Towards four in the afternoon we saw the McDonnell telegraph-station bungalow sitting comfortably on rising ground a mile ahead. There seemed no reason why we should not reach it within a short time, until we saw the great Skardon River running between us and the bungalow.

The Skardon is very beautiful and very deep in places; but, like the Dulhunty, it occasionally spreads its waters over flat rocky platforms, and we crossed it on one of these.

Mr. Evans, the linesman or the labourer, I am not sure which, had crossed the river to guide us. He instantly began a conversation on horse-racing, about which we know very little. . I told him so, but while we navvied the track down to the Skardon he carried on a rapid conversation about the ponies. Finally he said: "Look here, you fellows are going to spend a day or two with us, aren't you? "

I explained that we hardly dared to - that Cape York was now less than a hundred miles off, and that we were anxious to get there.

"Please stay - you might as well," he urged. "We don't see many people here, you know !"

I talked the matter over with Dick. The next day was Sunday; and so we both agreed to leave for Cape York on Monday. Mr. Evans was boyishly pleased when we told him.

But when a few minutes later we met good Mr. Hayes, he said, " It is needless for me to tell you boys how much I should like you both to spend a month with us; but you'd better push on in the morning. We've got three bags of flour left; you've got to take one for your aboriginals; until the rain comes and the grass grows, we cannot send a packhorse for more. If you don't take the flour, the blacks won't go with you to the Jardine. You've got to have them; you can't get to the Jardine alone," - Mr. Hayes became convincingly emphatic -" ou've got 'em now - the sooner you get away with them the better."

We saw the wisdom of this advice, and settled down to enjoy ourselves while we could.

Mr. Hayes has rosy cheeks and side whiskers.

He looks about fifty-six; he is actually nearly seventy.

He made a great fuss of us. He had made yeast bread and an ovenful of rich light scones and rock-cakes. From his store cupboard he had dug out all kinds of little dainties in the way of special kinds of cheese, biscuits, and fruit. He watched both of us as we ate, seeing to it that our plates were never empty.

And our boys were not forgotten. They were given a great feed of sweet potatoes, tea, and damper, and what was left over from our feast. We gave them a good ration of tobacco, and nothing was required to make them completely happy. After following the car all day, they should have been tired of the sight of her ; but they could not keep away from her while she was resting under the house, and the four of them slept beside her.

McDonnell, like Moreton, is a charming spot - plenty of tropical fruit and good vegetable gardens. Mr. Evans is an expert with pineapples as well as cabbages; we sampled both. The great pools in the Skardon are excellent for bathing, and during the dry season crocodiles are unknown. The trade winds blow across the bungalow compound, and McDonnell, according to Mr. Hayes - and I can well believe him - is a veritable health resort.

Mr. Hayes lent us the Fussles' great feather mattress, which we spread on the veranda. The result was a wonderful rest that night.

We were off the next morning soon after breakfast, now with Cape York a mere eighty miles ahead. Curiously, it now seemed farther off than it had been when we left Cooktown. I feel, however, that the final dash demands a fresh and a last chapter.

13

The Jardine!

THE country between McDonnell and a point some miles north of the great Jardine is curious and different. In other parts, where the soil is rich and fertile, there is no running water. Here the soil is poor and sandstoney rather than sandy, and creeks of sweet clear water run merrily even after months of dry weather. But the country thus naturally irrigated is so poor and unfruitful that it is not safe to travel with horses during the dry weather without carrying an impossible amount of fodder. Shortly after the rain begins, grass of a kind grows. Within the damp influence of these beautiful creeks, the ubiquitous gum-tree gives room to rich tropical scrub, palms, fern-trees, and immense, often sweet-smelling, trees whose names I do not know. A short distance from the creeks, the continuous march of eucalyptus forest recommences; and the land is baked hard.

Some miles north of McDonnell, we first met what is called locally the pitcher or jug plant I am out of my depth here, but the plant seemed to me a species of orchid, with all an orchid's cunning mechanics. The plant creeps to a certain extent, depending on other shrubs to support it. The pitcher is formed, I think, by what is really a true leaf rather than a blossom. But only a certain number of the leaves form pitchers. These are shaped precisely like an old-fashioned jug with a quaint little lip. They vary in size; and I noticed what I thought might be a dwarf species; but the usual size is about four inches long with a diameter of an inch. An extra spiral holds above the pitcher's mouth a neat little lid which will fit perfectly. During the wet season the lid comes down, and the vessel is sealed tight. The colour varies from dark green with a touch of purple to white.

A few insects are always found drowned in the water which the vessel invariably contains. This, I think, has led to the belief that the plant is carnivorous, that it actually lives on insect soup. My own impression is that the plant distills water from the air for its own use during the dry months, and that the dead insects are purely incidental. I think it was Mr. Armbruist who told us of a man who kept a pet pitcher-plant. He fed it on chunks of steak for many months until the pitcher assumed alarming proportions. Eventually he was forced to offer it fair-sized pigs for dinner. Obviously, he fell in himself one day, and was duly digested!

Although we had left McDonnell rather late in the morning, we made good progress that first day.

We crossed two or three creeks, but they were not very bad. Towards evening it began to rain gently and we looked at the sky with anxiety. But the boys reassured us. It would not be very much, they said ; and fortunately they were right. Nevertheless, without a tent it seemed as if we might have a very uncomfortable night if it continued to drizzle, until, with great ease, our men stripped wide sections of bark from suitable trees, and within a very short time we were sitting under an effective shelter.

When telling me that they proposed to make this shelter, Mickie said gently, "We must make a good house for our masters, so that we will have a good name on the road!" He took me aside some time later and tried to pump me regarding the amount of pay-off we proposed to give. "Good pay-off, Mickie," I replied, and he seemed quite satisfied.

Mr. Fussle was right. Without the blacks we should have had a sad and dangerous time. In many cases the deep central channels of the creeks we were now crossing had stout rustic bridges across them, made by the linesmen for their heavily laden packhorses; but the way down to a bridge and the way up from it were often impossible for us without much navvying.

Nolan Brook, the last creek before the great Jardine, ran along the surface without any valley to worry us. We simply crossed it on the bridge.

Nolan is notably charming. It is very deep, and occasionally forms gentle pool-like backwaters upon which float purple and cream water-lilies. The rustic bridge has good proportions, and the trees near the brook rise in conventional form. It was not difficult to imagine oneself in a park.

Towards the end of the day we began making a very gradual descent; the pad became very sandy and the telegraph-pole numbers assured us that we were approaching the great river, against which many people believed we could not prevail. Actually we were in its wet-weather bed, for the Jardine is several miles wide during the "wet." We must have disturbed an amorous brown snake somewhere about here, for he began chasing us. We did not see him, but Joe, hurrying behind us, saw him following our wheel-tracks, and killed him.

At five o'clock we reached the Jardine River. I recall looking across the great expanse of running water to the far bank, and saying to myself, "Ah - when once we are there!"

The Jardine is a good hundred and fifty yards wide, and during the dry season it runs over and between snowy white sandbanks. We had our plans made for the crossing, but an attempt could not be thought of that night.

When the boys rejoined us, Mickie led me down the river to the cattle ford. He said, "You and me go across and look him." I shuddered, but agreed. Unquestionably the Jardine is crocodile-infested, and if the reptiles had any courage no one would dare to ford the river. I could not allow myself to appear frightened before Mickie, and so we both waded in. Stockmen say that the Jardine is always a swim; but for once in its history it was unusually and agreeably low. The sand was very soft and unpleasant, but we were never in water above our armpits. Our progress was distressingly slow, and it occurred to me half-way across that a shy crocodile might become bold at any minute. The current was swift, but not actually swift enough to knock a man down. I discovered that the river shoaled very badly near the far bank and that the sand in this shallow water was quicksand. One sunk up to one's knees and the withdrawal of feet was difficult.

After a few minutes' examination of the far bank, Mickie and I began the return crossing. I was chatting gaily with him, but my nerves were on edge. I recalled how people had said that crocodiles need not bother one at the Jardine because the water is so clear that they could be seen coming. I estimated the speed of a crocodile at thirty miles an hour in the water; Mickie's and my own utmost speed was perhaps one mile per hour. It seemed to me that a crocodile would have it all his own way if he made a rush at us when we were anything more than three feet from the bank. I must admit that I was seriously scared, and that I hurried, not easy in running water never below one's waist. Dick, I may say, was at the telegraph clearing two hundred yards higher up the river.

It was most unfortunate that he should decide to practise with his revolver by shooting at a black stump floating down with the current at the moment when Mickie and I were in midstream. I heard the shots in rapid succession, and I decided at once that a crocodile was his target, and that the reptile was tearing downstream. Obviously, I decided, it would pick me up *en route*.

At the first bang I jumped from the water. "My hat, a crocodile!" I yelled; and jumped higher at the next shot. Mickie nearly collapsed in the stream with merriment. I was not altogether reassured; but I thought it best to laugh, too, and to make many more little bounds from the rushing water to show Mickie that I was doing it merely for fun. He was not deceived.

That night, before turning in, we made our plans for the crossing. I would leave the camp two hours before dawn and go with the boys two miles back along the clearing to a spot where cypress pine grew. All the timber near the Jardine is hardwood and will not float. We would return with as much timber as possible.. Dick would drive to the cattle ford and there dismantle the car, removing the battery, the magneto, the carburettor, and what cushions could be removed. (The prospect on Thursday Island had to be thought of!)

This worked out well to the point when the raft was completed. But then we discovered that while the raft would hold Mickie if he stood very still, it would not hold Mickie plus Charlie. The cypress pine would float, but it seemed to have as much as it could do to keep itself afloat without bothering about any further burden. It certainly could not hold the car. Then Dick saw that I had placed the main logs across the raft instead of lengthways, and, deciding that it might be a case of occasionally pushing the raft along the bottom, he thought it best to make an alteration which meant pulling my craft to pieces. This was not difficult; she was held together by telegraph wire!

Finally we hit upon an ingenious idea. The McDonnell folks keep a small dinghy at the river for ferrying stores across. This was chained and locked to a tree, and in a very leaky condition. It was much too small to take the car. But the buoyancy of even this small boat was infinitely greater than any raft we could make; and so we decided to borrow the dinghy by chopping down the branch to which it was chained. Then we made shafts-long, stout poles bound along the length of the raft and projecting the length of the dinghy.

We backed the dinghy in between the shafts and lashed her firmly, under and over. Then we placed two long stout poles across the stern of the raft for the boys to hold, to keep the stern buoyant.

The raft had her stern aground at the edge of the bank and her bow was held up well by the dinghy, which incidentally had to be kept baled.

The car descending to the raft at the Jardine River.

Half-way across the Jardine River

The car ran obligingly on to the raft and was securely lashed to it. The dinghy took the weight easily.

But when once we had pushed into deep water and the stern had left the bank, our situation seemed most precarious. For while the dinghy held up well, the boys and I could not keep the stern far from the bottom of the river. I would have suggested a pause for more thought; but Dick took up a position at the dinghy and said, "Come on, now - let's get across !"

If Mickie, Joe, Charlie, and Peter had been capable of concerted action, all might have been well; but it happened that Mickie and Joe on the port side tired at a moment when Charlie and Peter were lifting. Thus Charlie's and Peter's side would often rise dangerously when Mickie's and Joe's sunk, and often the car threatened to topple. Then Charlie and Joe would lose courage, and down would go the stern of the raft to the sand, the Baby's bonnet emerging in an attitude of supplication from the rushing water.

The only thing to do was to shout and shriek, even to make bad jokes - anything, to keep the boys going. I sang songs and yelled for some dozen yards with great success, until I made a shocking *faux pas*. I shouted, "Come on Mickie and Joe - give her ten - whoop!"

Mickie and Joe responded magnificently; but Charlie and Peter did not. Uprose the Baby's port side dripping with water; down went her starboard side! The car trembled, threatening to topple over, but righted herself in time. It was a trying moment!

"What's the joke? " Dick shouted icily; "you want to capsize the car, do you? - very funny!" I believe he was seriously annoyed; but I could think of nothing sufficiently rude to fling back at that moment.

Besides, my thoughts were occupied with crocodiles. The current was rushing against us - especially when, eventually, we were forced to turn into its teeth to avoid a shoal in front of us! After a time the boys seemed to give up trying to keep their end up, and it became a matter of pushing the stern of the raft along the sand, which was dangerously soft. Altogether it was an exceedingly difficult and dangerous operation, which succeeded more by good fortune than by anything else.

Dick, who, from the moment he took hold of the dinghy at the near bank never ceased to pull with all his strength until the far bank was reached, tells me that his greatest trouble was thirst, which seems absurd in view of the fact that he was in water often up to 'his shoulders; he dared not release an ounce of strength to bend to drink ! Frankly, in his place, I would have taken one or two gulps!

After a fight of two full hours against soft sand and the current, we ran against the far bank, and thanked God. During those hours there was not a minute which did not contain serious risk. The boys were as pleased as we were to get across, and immediately danced a dance of joy.

We paid off our men when again we were on the telegraph clearing. Mickie called it "the best pay-off in the whole world!" It was certainly the most interesting-old pipes, three safety razors which had reached the expensive stage of cutting more strops than they should, bachelor's buttons, pencils, tobacco, old coats, much flour, tea, sugar, and tobacco- and a few shillings each to clinch the business with. When at last we bade them goodbye and they cried, we both felt a tightening in the region of the throat; we had all become great friends. Joe, who had learned to regard Dick as a great hero, was particularly affected and burst into tears, rather like a small boy in trouble - "Dood-bye, Dit-dood-bye, Dit-oo-yowl-oo-ogord "

I fear that I have not offered much information about the blacks of the Peninsula. I cannot, with any degree of truth. We saw very little of them, for there are not now many left in the land through which the telegraph passes.

On then with less than forty miles before us.

There were two hours of daylight left in that fair day; and we hoped to cover ten miles. But, alas, turkey-brush gave us six punctures in rapid succession and we were forced to camp hardly more than two miles north of the Jardine.

Turkey-brush is a very pretty sage-like scrub which seldom grows higher than four or five feet. Its twigs and small branches have the capacity of steel to pierce rubber, and even leather, we were told. Few horses will face turkey-brush willingly. We discovered, too, that if we carried on for more than a yard after a puncture, the twig, piercing the outer cover, tore great rents in the inner tube. It looked very bad for that prospect on Thursday Island! We reached close to the necessity of stuffing the tyres with grass or sand, which would have been a great pity, because the little car was still otherwise in perfect condition.

We hardly ate that night ; and we hardly slept.

Thirty-eight miles separated us from Cape York. Should we get there? Could we? Until that night we had never doubted our ability to reach the end of Australia. Now it seemed almost impossible.

But hope came at dawn, when we were ready to start. We had all the tyres tight, and three or four good hours of coolness before us. Alas, we had only travelled three hundred yards when flat went a tyre. Having mended this, we proceeded - but, to make a sad story short, I had better say at once that at the ninth puncture, with only four miles covered, we were seriously discouraged. Discouragement was a new sensation to us; we had not known it before. Hot day with its offering of small flies was upon us.

But fortunately, after the ninth puncture, the turkey-brush ceased, and we began making excellent progress.

Petrol was now becoming scarce. Only good luck, we were amazed to find, would get us through.

We reached the neighbourhood of Red Island, where the Fresh Food and Ice Company of Thursday Island slaughter beasts. It was the first sign of our renewed connection with the outer world. We found a Japanese charcoal burner called Tokita, who gave us tea and pineapples. We ran the mile down Tokita's road to the sea; but the glory of the blueness of the Gulf of Carpentaria meant little to us that day.

Going a little farther north and branching off from the pad, we called in at the Red Island slaughteryard, and told that very good soul, Mrs. Gibson - I must mention her - that we were short of petrol.

"I've got plenty," she said, and instantly produced six bottles of the precious fluid. She uses petrol for her iron. It was natural enough for Mrs. Gibson to have petrol, but very lucky that she had but newly accumulated a fresh store. It seemed a miracle to us.

On then for Cape York!

Cape York was less than twenty miles ahead of us; and we had every chance of getting there before dark. But a very bad creek called Takanau less than nine miles south of our journey's end, held us up for some hours, and, when we were free of Takanau, it was getting dark.

We should have camped; we could not!

Indeed we had hardly eaten that day. Flinging caution to the wind, we struggled on in the dark. I can hear at this moment that brave little British engine singing away as sweetly as she had sung in Sydney. Sometimes she had to struggle very seriously over the pad, which was becoming more sandy as time passed, but she never failed us. I was walking twenty yards ahead with an electric torch, giving Dick warning of stumps, ant-heaps, and water-courses. The sand here is the home of many small death-adders effectively camouflaged white and grey, but no death-adder crossed my path. I can still see the little car's brilliant headlights swinging this way and that across the great avenue which forms the telegraph clearing; and I can easily recall the joy I felt when at last they lit up some sliprails ahead of us.

"Sliprails, Dick," I called, "we shall soon be there!"

I heard no reply; the little engine was still singing sweetly; the Baby was bobbing and creeping her confident way like a clever insect along the pad. She seemed, quite unconcerned. I might have been amazed had she suddenly given tongue and said, "What's all this fuss about? I can get there all right!" But if she had said, "Well - what's the big idea, anyway? What did you lead me here for?" I should have been puzzled to find an answer.

We reached the sliprails and entered the home paddock of Cape York telegraph station. We crept over very soft sand for some time; and then that avenue of thousands of miles ended abruptly.

We saw lights in a house; we honked our horn; soon a little pool of brilliant light came dancing over the ground towards us. It was Mr. Gunn, the postmaster, watching his steps with an electric torch; Mr. Gunn knows his local death-adders!

Finally we reached a sand-mound, the most northerly end of Australia, and stopped. Dick got out of the car and took my hand.

"Thank God! " he said.

"Thank God! " I said.

Publisher's note: The author did sell the Baby to a party on Thursday Island, and the Austin 7 company gave the authors a new Baby Austin for a world trip; published as *Round the World in a Baby Austin* **(ETT Imprint, 2025).**

www.ingramcontent.com/pod-product-compliance
Lightning Source LLC
Chambersburg PA
CBHW020804160426
43192CB00006B/430